Also by Bryan M. Chavis

Buy It, Rent It, Profit!

THE LANDLORD ENTREPRENEUR

DOUBLE YOUR PROFITS WITH REAL ESTATE PROPERTY MANAGEMENT

BRYAN M. CHAVIS

TOUCHSTONE

NEW YORK   LONDON   TORONTO   SYDNEY   NEW DELHI

Touchstone
An Imprint of Simon & Schuster, Inc.
1230 Avenue of the Americas
New York, NY 10020

First Touchstone trade paperback edition September 2017

TOUCHSTONE and colophon are registered trademarks of Simon & Schuster, Inc.

For information about special discounts for bulk purchases, please contact Simon & Schuster Special Sales at 1-866-506-1949 or business@simonandschuster.com.

The Simon & Schuster Speakers Bureau can bring authors to your live event. For more information or to book an event, contact the Simon & Schuster Speakers Bureau at 1-866-248-3049 or visit our website at www.simonspeakers.com.

Manufactured in the United States of America

1 3 5 7 9 10 8 6 4 2

Library of Congress Cataloging-in-Publication Data

Names: Chavis, Bryan, 1972– author.
Title: The landlord entrepreneur : double your profits with real estate property management / by Bryan M. Chavis.
Description: New York : Touchstone, 2017. | Includes index.
Identifiers: LCCN 2017015228 (print) | LCCN 2017030880 (ebook) | ISBN 9781501147203 (Ebook) | ISBN 9781501147180 (pbk.)
Subjects: LCSH: Real estate management. | Rental housing. | Real estate investment. | Landlord and tenant.
Classification: LCC HD1394 (ebook) | LCC HD1394 .C453 2017 (print) | DDC 333.5068—dc23
LC record available at https://lccn.loc.gov/2017015228

ISBN 978-1-5011-4718-0
ISBN 978-1-5011-4720-3 (ebook)

I dedicate this book to my wonderful family, my wife, Lacy, and my beautiful daughter, Naomi.

CONTENTS

INTRODUCTION

If you've read my first book, *Buy It, Rent It, Profit!*, you may know a little bit about my background in real estate. But in case you haven't, I'll give you the condensed version: I've been working in the apartment industry, where I received my Certified Apartment Manager (CAM) designation, for more than twenty years. I started my career by managing large rental complexes, and I later became an owner, investing in my own multifamily units.

I've become an expert in the industry, publishing a bestselling book, speaking to thousands of people all around the world, and personally coaching other people just like you, who want to find their own success and financial freedom in the real estate industry. Perhaps most important in my career, though, has been the development of The Landlord Academy (www.landlordacademy.com), an online destination that takes all of the things that I've learned throughout my decades in the industry—all the tips, tricks, best practices, and systems—and distills them into educational, training, and coaching resources that remove the guesswork from real estate entrepreneurship. But if you visit The Landlord Academy, you may be surprised to find that there isn't a lot of information about real estate investing. Instead, my focus is on teaching potential entrepreneurs about the highly lucrative field of property management.

Through my company The Landlord Property Management Academy, I have helped thousands of real estate investors, agents, and brokers create property management businesses. My experience has allowed me a rare inside look at how most start-up businesses approach real estate investing and property management. I have found that while most licensed real estate professionals have all the licensing required by law to practice real estate, most lack the skill sets to create and operate a successful business. Most have the mind-set that a license will provide all the credibility and skills. Unfortunately, many of the licensing schools and seminars these professionals have gone through provide them with resources that often fall short when it comes to developing the individual as a business owner. They fail to provide not only useful industry knowledge but the guidance and systems needed to operate a successful business.

When you call yourself a real estate agent or landlord, you are categorizing yourself in a way that keeps you from being held accountable. An agent might blame the broker, the broker might blame economic conditions, the investor might blame the contractor.

When you call yourself an entrepreneur, you are taking responsibility for the success of business. Everything begins and ends with you. The business owner is ultimately responsible for the entire company. In all of my experience working with these individuals, I have found the entrepreneurs to be more successful because of this mind-set. Accountability, self-discipline, perseverance, and adaptation are of the highest importance in this industry. In this book, I will provide you with the knowledge, guidance, and systems that are needed to make your property management business a success.

The Landlord Entrepreneur Needs:

- Communication skills
- Interpersonal skills
- Professionalism
- Organizational skills
- Detail-oriented mind-set
- Analytic mind-set
- Knowledge of financial basics
- Leadership skills
- Ability to grasp basic economic concepts
- Good understanding of technology
- Ability to adapt

PART I

PROPERTY MANAGEMENT AND THE NEW REAL ESTATE ENTREPRENEURS

UNDERSTANDING THE VALUE WITHIN THE REAL ESTATE INDUSTRY

Property management as the foundation of real estate investing

As a real estate professional or investor, you know firsthand how cyclical the real estate market can be at times. I'm often asked, "Is there a foolproof plan to always generating cash flow in real estate no matter the market?" The answer is yes. The plan, or business, is property management. Management at the on-site level is a staple of the industry; the need for property management on the operational level makes it virtually volatile proof. Property management also provides what most businesses need and strive for: cash flow and passive income.

Before we dive deeper into the value of property management within the real estate industry, let's take a look at the three segments of real estate, which most people identify with from a commercial real estate perspective.

Three Segments of Real Estate

- **Residential**: Single-family or multifamily property that is used for occupation purposes
- **Commercial**: Nonresidential property used for business purposes only, including stores, malls, office space
- **Industrial**: Land or buildings used for industrial purposes, including manufacturing, warehousing, and research

Understand that within residential, there is a commercial aspect. Why is the term *commercial* used within the residential segment? The answer is that rental housing is often considered commercial after exceeding four units. Property management companies often identify all their rental properties the same way, but the complexities of the investment property change as more units are added. Economies of scales, interactions with contractors and vendors, and insurance requirements all change. Most of all, skill sets will need to change. Both single-unit rentals and multifamily-type assets are looked at as investments. How does all of this fit into your property management business? There are four standard focuses for a property management business:

Residential: Typically, a property management business that's focusing on residential will look to manage single-family homes and small portfolios of single-family rental homes. A property management company with a focus on residential may also specialize in vacation rentals as well as possibly managing vacant homes. A residential manager must focus on many processes; however, one process in particular will prove to be vital: the process of tenant screening. Although tenant screening is important for all property managers, there is an increased importance on single-family rentals as there is only one source of income to pay down expenses.

Most property management clients/investors transition to small or midsize apartment buildings to receive the benefit of economies of scale. To illustrate this, consider that as a property management business you have two investors: one with a single-family home, and the other with a duplex. If both investors have one vacancy, the single-family home investor is 100 percent vacant and the duplex investor is 50 percent vacant. The duplex investor is benefiting from the economies of scale by owning one more unit, thereby reducing risk by 50 percent. The skills needed to lease rental units and qualified tenants are extremely important to the single-family property management business model.

Residential/Commercial: This describes a property management company that focuses on renting a hybrid of single-family homes and commercial-grade rental assets. As I stated before, property management companies begin to define their rental properties as commercial grade when the rental units exceed more than four units. There are differences in how a portfolio of single-family homes should operate versus one of commercial-grade assets. These are described in detail later in the book. For example, if you are managing a portfolio of single-family homes, those homes may not be located in the same city. Whereas if you are dealing with apartment buildings, all of the units would be located in one general area. Managing a portfolio spread out throughout various zip codes requires time-management skills as well as a high level of dependency on reliable vendors. With midsize apartment buildings, the management of tenants as well as the management of vendors is typically easier. On the flip side of the coin, when dealing with a single-family rental portfolio a skilled property manager will create a lease that puts most of the responsibility of day-to-day operations on the tenant rather than the property manager.

The property management business that focuses on a hybrid portfolio must define the qualifying criteria, rules and regulations, and the process for screening tenants. Accomplishing this will mitigate vacancies and costly evictions. You can find sample qualifying criteria template forms within this book, as well as many other must-have forms.

Commercial/Retail: There are differences between dealing with a business versus a tenant. When dealing with retail, a property management company's primary concern is risk management. These property management companies put in place what is known as a triple-net lease. This lease typically places the majority of responsibilities to maintain the premises that the business occupies—aside from the common areas—on the actual tenant.

Industrial: This sector includes buildings slated for industrial use, such as manufacturing, production, assembly, storage, and distribution. I see this sector as a growth sector, as consumers move from purchasing items from traditional brick-and-mortar stores to patronizing businesses such as Amazon and others that are looking to level up their online sales. This is already spurring the growth of this sector of real estate.

LOOK FOR OPPORTUNITIES

I have personally chosen to focus on the residential segment of the real estate industry. Through fluctuations in the economy, I have seen people cut their Starbucks budget, I have seen people go without cable TV, I have even seen people sell their car and buy a bike. However, housing is one of the last things that people can go without. For this reason, I see stability and a bit of insulation from economic cycles that affect most sectors of real estate investing. The real estate industry cycles are influenced by micro and macro changes to economic health within the nation, demographic changes, interest rates, employment, and legislation. The lower- and middle-income demographics are directly tied to these influences of economic cycles. As long as there is a need for housing, there is a need for a property manager. I have often said that it is one of the oldest professions in history; property management is even mentioned in the Bible: Jesus was born in a manger, and that manger was operated by the innkeeper . . . aka a landlord.

THE GLUE THAT HOLDS THE INVESTMENT TOGETHER

Property management is the glue that holds the segments of the real estate investment industry together. Property management businesses have evolved tremendously for most, from being a standard rent collector to more of a business consultant. To clarify, property management companies are evolving from managing rental property to managing their clients' businesses. These businesses involve the management of portfolios ranging from single-family homes and midsized apartment buildings to industrial complexes and mixed-use developments. It's the combination of managing real property, businesses, people, and, oh yeah, let's not forget vendors/contractors as well.

So on any given day, the property manager can be managing multiple relationships as well as the actual physical property itself. This takes not only the efforts of highly skilled and trained individuals, but also the employment of successful operating systems to provide a consistent and predictable service to all. In my experience, only through system predictability and consistency can a business obtain profitability.

Most brokerages are set up now with a focus on transactions. This type of brokerage's ability to generate income is greatly impacted by the fluctuations in the real estate industry.

HOW TECHNOLOGY HAS TRANSFORMED THE CONVENTIONAL REAL ESTATE BROKERAGE

Technology is disrupting transaction-focused brokerages. I began to identify and understand these threats as I introduced property management as a source of income to real estate brokerages. Listening to how most brokerages wanted to grow their business and how most were concerned about the impact technology would have on one day reducing their commissions or eventually eliminating them altogether, I realized there had to be a better way. It was time for me to create a real estate brokerage that focused on managing not only my investment group's assets but the assets of others as well. I began to see a trend emerging, a trend that would be heavily reliant on the property management industry, so like any entrepreneur I had to act on this vision.

After meeting with many highly qualified brokers, I still felt that I wasn't really on the path to what I saw as the brokerage of the future. Finally, I met with one of my youngest coaching clients, Nathan, the head of business development with our Academy. Along with our licensing and franchising attorney, as well as a host of other real estate business leaders, we realized collectively that there had to be a better way to do our jobs. That new way of looking at real estate investing led us to coin a new term, as well as a new business model—one that anyone could apply and succeed with. But you won't yet find this new term in any dictionary:

resimercial (rez-i-MUR-shl), adj.: bringing together residential and commercial real estate in a flawless systematic approach to creating wealth by beginning in residential investments and progressing to commercial real estate investments

Our group set out to bridge the gap between residential and commercial real estate. There was not a clear path for the noninstitutional-grade investor to enter the market and grow. It is very common for an investor to work with real estate agents who are strictly sales oriented, meaning that they could not help the investor develop customized investment strategies. We found this unacceptable, knowing that most investors are noninstitutional investors, meaning they don't yet own a large portfolio of rentals. There was a need for a professional who would be a hybrid form of a residential agent and a commercial broker. That need drove us to create the *resimercial* system. My hope is that you see the same need either as a beginning entrepreneur looking for your first real estate venture, or as a seasoned real estate professional looking to change with the times.

ENTRY TO PROPERTY MANAGEMENT: BUILD YOUR EMPIRE FROM THE GROUND UP

If you are reading this book, you may be finding yourself at a crossroads. Whether you were laid off from your job, are graduating from high school or college, or are looking for a career change, first let me say from personal experience: never despise humble beginnings. Second, wisely consider your options. When considering a career in real estate, the barriers to entry are focused on skills, and the ability to obtain knowledge and skills, rather than on money. These days you can start your company with minimal debt. With the constant emergence of new technology, you don't necessarily have to buy into a costly franchise to get the infrastructure and systems required for start-up. You don't have to go to college, only spend the next ten-plus years working yourself out of debt. With hard work and smart decisions, virtually anyone can become a financially successful real estate entrepreneur. There are countless stories of people starting with nothing and building an empire.

USING THE SHARED ECONOMY TO JUMP-START YOUR BUSINESS

There are many definitions of the shared economy. The concept has been around for years. Peer-to-peer trade has always been important to economies. The major difference in today's time is once again . . . the impact of technology. These goods and services can be utilized and shared in ways previously not possible. The shared economy allows you to utilize your resources more efficiently. The current cost of starting and operating a business is far less than it was for previous generations.

When starting a real estate brokerage, we can leverage shared economies to reduce overhead. In the very beginning at Chavis Realty, we weighed the costs and benefits against our start-up expenses. We found we were able to deliver a higher level of service with less expense and oversight. We decided to save money by utilizing virtual office space, a virtual receptionist, virtual assistants, and a virtual bookkeeper. These shared economy small business hacks allowed us to address our daily functions as a property management business while scaling back our costs. This book will teach you how to develop a business plan and provide you with a sample operations manual and marketing packet to guide you toward operating a successful property management company.

Property management has been a tremendous benefit in our lives and we want to share those benefits. Here are a few of the shared economy platforms we are currently using:

- Office space: Regus office rentals, www.regus.com
- Project management software: Basecamp, www.basecamp.com
- Virtual receptionists: Ruby Receptionists, www.callruby.com

---

Requirements of the Property Management Business

- *A product:* Normally a business has a product; businesses look to develop that product and anticipate its future needs. In property management the properties need to be constantly evaluated to make sure they are fitting the client's overall goals.
- *Team processes:* For interviewing, selecting, hiring, training, supervising
- *Legal requirements:* Compliance with laws and licensing requirements
- *Financial requirements:* Operating funds as well as bookkeeping processes are created and followed
- *Protection:* Maintenance of the property itself, protection of cash flow (NOI, net operating income), ultimately protecting long-term value
- *Emergency/risk management:* Policies are put in place to address crisis situations for the property and tenant, and a client's exposure to risk, as well as the neighborhoods in which the investment properties are located
- *Marketing:* Developed based on the strategic evaluation of the targeted area (SEOTA) as well as comprehensive market surveys that periodically change based on economic conditions
- *Customer relations:* Understanding needs of tenants and clients and fulfillment of those needs

---

BRYAN'S STORY

If you have heard me speak at a conference, give a lecture, or viewed one of my YouTube training videos, you've often heard me talk about what it takes to become a successful entrepreneur. Now, I know there are a lot of self-proclaimed experts on this topic out there; every week there seems to be a new thought leader giving us their take on "five things every entrepreneur needs to know," so I will spare you the shortcuts. Truthfully, there are none.

The only path I know to success as an entrepreneur is riddled with obstacles and setbacks. However, if you acquire the skill sets you will need to survive and advance, the payoffs will be even greater than you imagined.

I have learned a lot over the past several years since my last book, *Buy It, Rent It, Profit!,* was published. About what it takes to be successful with very little cash, help, or, frankly, even less motivation to keep trying. I know what it takes to keep moving forward in the face of adversity; I started my career as an entrepreneur with only a high school diploma . . . did I mention a special education diploma at that? Yes, I rode the short bus to school, lol; however, I did not let my learning disabilities stop me or define me.

I also know all too well what it's like to look at a stack of bills and then look at my bank account and see an overdrawn account. I have very personal experience of doing everything right but yet still waking up every day to new obstacles, each more challenging than those the day before. But none of these challenges could have prepared me for what I would face at the end of 2012.

On Christmas Eve of 2012 I was rushed to the hospital after having a seizure. I was diagnosed with a brain tumor. There is good news and bad news with this story. The bad news was that the tumor was located close to my motor cortex. This was why I was having focal-related seizures. The good news was that there were few cancerous cells and it was more of a solid mass. I spent the next two years battling chemo and weekly seizures, which caused crippling pain in the left side of my body and extreme sickness. Keep in mind I still had to work—in fact, most of the YouTube videos of me stabilizing apartment buildings were shot while I was going through chemo. I understand what it's like to have a seizure in the hotel room forty-five minutes before having to give an eight-hour lecture on property management.

Seeing that the location of the tumor was so close to my motor cortex, most surgeons said it was too risky to try to remove it, as doing so would most likely paralyze me on my left side and I could lose the ability to speak. When I finally found a doctor willing to remove the tumor— shout-out to Dr. Valley and Dr. Jugal—I had to be awake for most of the brain surgery so they could see just how much of my speech and motor skills I would lose. To make a long story short, the surgery went well and I fought successfully to regain my motor skills and speech. I'm often asked how I did it; let's just say that's for another book. But I will say this much: nothing is imposable with *faith*.

The story gets worse before it gets better. Anyone who has battled any extreme illness will know that if the sickness doesn't kill you, the medical bills will. I am going to point out how property management helped get me through this difficult time in my life and on the path to recovery. The seizures and chemo treatments prohibited me from being able to travel and perform the speaking engagements that accounted for a large portion of my income. At this point in my life, I had never had so much as a cavity. I was an athlete. I saw the importance of insuring my real estate but not, unfortunately, of insuring myself. With speaking being very lucrative, I was spoiled. Having my brand as a speaker temporarily stripped from me, I was forcibly reminded of how fundamentally sound a property management business is.

My negative circumstances allowed for a positive seed to be planted; it was time for me to go back to my fundamentals and start a property management company once again, but this time I would look to manage others' investments as well, not just my own. Knowing that hard times never last, that there is a season for all aspects of life, a season for struggle, a season for pain, a season for learning about one's self, and yes, a season for starting over and coming back stronger. I would finance this comeback with the help of property management.

It was time to cofound a new type of real estate brokerage, one that would be deeply rooted in property management, and understand the true meaning of value as it pertains to real estate investor clients. As you're reading this book, you may be yourself facing some sort of challenge, you may be broke right now, just barely able to pay for this book, you may be a single parent, you may be stuck in a dead-end job, there may be a Goliath that you must slay. No matter your challenge, I want you to remember, as I said in the acknowledgments of this book, that *impossible* is a big word on the tips of the tongues of small-minded men who lack faith, the faith in one's self to overcome what others say is impossible. If impossible were a fact, then I would not have been around to write this book. Impossible is nothing more than a word.

ELLIE'S STORY

Ellie is a doctor, and by all accounts he's pretty successful already. But he wants to move into radiology, which means he'll need more studies and another residency. Additionally, he'll have to take a drastic pay cut while he's working toward his new career, but once he becomes a radiologist, his current income (around $200,000) will double. In the meantime, though, Ellie reached out to me because he was thinking about buying a duplex or other property so that he could create another revenue stream while he's back in school. But, he added, he has a wife and two children, so he can't afford to do anything stupid.

So what does Ellie's story have to do with property management? Everything, actually.

Ellie reached out to me because he was looking for a set-it-and-forget-it way to make money while his doctor income took a hit. He figured that if he bought some property and quickly threw in some tenants, he'd have cash rolling in while he studied radiology. Basically, he didn't view real estate investing as a real *business*—a business that, more than anything else, requires property management. Individuals who have become successful real estate investors have also had to become successful property managers—or they've had to outsource their property management needs to another person or company. Without learning how to work with tenants, for example, it's impossible to make a significant return on your investment.

You wouldn't open up a restaurant without taking the time to understand all of the roles that need to be filled in order for the business to function properly and then hiring the right people to fill those roles. You wouldn't ignore all the legal aspects of your fast-food business, thus failing to protect yourself from, say, a lady who spills coffee on her lap bringing a lawsuit against you. You also wouldn't overlook the industry at large and neglect to incorporate the best practices of your competitors. Those missteps would cause your business to fail almost as quickly as it launched. And if you embark on real estate investing without treating it like a true business—thereby gaining an understanding of the integral role of property management—the fate of your business will be just as drastic.

Once I explained this to Ellie, he got it immediately. He adopted more of an entrepreneurial approach to his real estate ventures and asked me to teach him everything I knew about property management. I walked him through everything I'm going to teach you in this book. And here's the best part: Once Ellie learned everything he needed to know to manage his own property, he saw how easy it was to apply those same systems to managing the properties of other people. So instead of just making an extra $1,500 per month renting out his duplex, he made an extra $5,000 per month renting out his duplex *and* selling his property management services to other real estate investors.

THE GIMMICK BEHIND THE MILLIONAIRE MIND-SET

Ellie's story is not unique. I've spoken to a lot of people at seminars and conferences around the country, I've personally coached others, and I've read book reviews on Amazon. People want real estate riches without starting a real estate *business*.

I wrote an entire book on real estate investing, and I've been an investor myself, so I understand that some people are naturally drawn to this segment of the industry. But what I always try to get people to understand is this: You are an entrepreneur. Real estate investing is what you *do*, it's not who you *are*. If you have even one renter, you are an entrepreneur who owns real estate *and* a property management company.

I see a lot of people who sell themselves short and dumb themselves down by calling themselves a "landlord" as opposed to an "entrepreneur." They get away with treating themselves like a non-entrepreneur, so they don't take themselves too seriously. And, as a result, their businesses aren't as successful as they could be. But if, like Ellie, you start adopting an entrepreneurial mind-set—whether you're a real estate investor first, or just getting started with property management—your financial possibilities are endless. In *Buy It, Rent It, Profit!*, I taught people how to buy an investment property, but in this book, I'm teaching you how to be a business owner. I'm going to teach you how to operate and maintain that investment—whether it's your investment or someone else's.

Let me drill down on the last point for a minute. I can go on and on about the benefits and income potential of a property management company, but unless you establish a real business that is reputable in the eyes of your potential clients, the possibilities I've spoken about will always remain out of reach. Sure, you'll be able to manage your own properties, but you won't be able to achieve the growth, scale, and nearly risk-free business potential that you can when you manage the properties of others.

I've sat in countless meetings with multimillionaire investors, and they all have one thing in common: They know the value of good property management. They know that even if they've spent millions upon millions of dollars to build out their investment portfolios, if those properties are managed by people who haven't been properly trained and don't understand the proper systems and procedures of property management, their properties will essentially be run into the ground, causing them to lose tremendous value on their assets.

They don't have time to read books like this one, or to learn how to manage their properties themselves, so they look for the best of the best in order to outsource that responsibility. Even though they aren't on the ground actually managing properties, these millionaire investors are very management savvy. They look for property managers who are trained well and who will take great care of their properties so that they can treat those individuals like family and pay them well.

This is the exact opposite of what I see when I attend real estate investment club meetings, where there are a bunch of people who are still trying to become rich. Like Ellie, they think it's all about buying the property, and that once they figure out some clever financing techniques and purchase a few single-family homes, they'll be millionaires in no time. They see the value in the properties, but they don't understand that a well-managed property can create more value that can later be translated into more properties with even greater growth potential.

As you build your property management company, you are going to want to work with people in the first group—the multimillionaire investors who know the importance of high-quality property management services. But the caveat is that those individuals will not work with you if you don't have a solid business that they can entrust their assets to.

I'm going to walk you step-by-step through the process of building a property management business from scratch. I'm going to show you people who are successful, so you can see how they've built their companies, then I'm going to teach you how to execute your property management services on a day-to-day basis, as well as how to land those clients I just talked about. According to the popular saying, "If you fail to plan, you plan to fail," and I couldn't agree with that more. By the time you finish reading this book, you will have a complete business plan, as well as all of the forms, contracts, and agreements you'll need in your business. This is as turnkey as it gets, and I'm giving all of this to you because I know what's possible for you if you just have the tools you need.

THE THREE MOST IMPORTANT THINGS TO LEARN ABOUT HOW TO PROFIT IN THE REAL ESTATE INDUSTRY

SEOTA process from the property manager's perspective

Even if you are a beginner in real estate, you've heard the cliché "Location, location, location." Well, location is obviously key, but you have to think differently when you're dealing with rental properties. A nice neighborhood with rising home values may be a good location to buy a home in, but it may not necessarily be an attractive area to acquire rental investments. This is why professional property managers know how to advise their investor clients on which sort of rental investments will fit their client's specific needs. They do this by performing what I teach as the SEOTA process.

WHAT IS THE SEOTA PROCESS? AND HOW DOES A PROPERTY MANAGER USE IT TO HELP CLIENTS?

SEOTA stands for the Strategic Evaluation of a Target Area, a step-by-step process for evaluating a property and determining whether it's a good investment. In this chapter, I will explain how the SEOTA process should work for the property manager. Successful implementation will set you apart from the competition. In this chapter, you will learn how to strategically evaluate target areas for real estate investments, how to analyze the deals financially, the difference between different types of investment "asset classes," and finally, the five phases of real estate investing.

HOW THE SEOTA PROCESS IS USED BY THE PROPERTY MANAGER

The SEOTA process is used not only to help identify target areas for potential real estate investments, but also during the property analysis. Let's first start with what is a property analysis and how it is used. A property analysis is used to help identify the property's strengths and weaknesses, but it is also used to help determine:

- Management agreement: This is the agreement or contract between you and the client. Understanding that not every property will operate the same, the property manager will use the SEOTA to help set up the basics of the property analysis, which will include setting up the properties.
- Property qualifying criteria
- Property rules and regulations
  - Lease contract
  - Rental rates
  - Late fees
  - Management fees

Understanding that no two properties will necessarily run on the same qualifying criteria (depending on their location and the demographics of the neighborhood), you will set up your analysis of the property accordingly, as well as your management agreement covering the fees and level of services the management company will offer. As a quick example: You will notice that items on the shelves of box stores such as Walmart will change from zip code to zip code. This is because the demographics of people change from zip code to zip code. The same applies to rental property. What rents on one side of town may not rent on the other side. Also, you may be facing more operational challenges with properties located in certain neighborhoods. A good property management company will often account for such challenges and have that reflected in the fee offered to manage the property. We will go more in depth on this when we cover the day-to-day operation systems of a property management business.

STEP 1: HELP YOUR CLIENTS FIND THE OPPORTUNITIES FOR RENTAL INVESTMENTS THROUGH THE STRATEGIC EVALUATION OF A TARGET AREA

The first goal of the SEOTA process is to identify areas that are good rental markets for your clients. Once completed, the information is assembled to provide a clear picture of who the potential tenants are and what their perceived needs are. This process allows users to see areas of opportunity in advance.

SEOTA, Key Indicators Broken Down Step-by-Step

When you perform the SEOTA analysis, you will be taking a look at key demographic and economic indicators that reveal whether or not an area is worth investing in. These indicators are:

1. Building permits
2. Employment
3. Average household size
4. Demographics
5. Psychographics
6. Mortgage interest rates
7. Rental market rates
8. Occupancy rates

Let's take a closer look at them:

1. *Building permits.* A property manager will look at building permits to help track growth. We evaluate the various types of building permits—for single-family homes, multifamily homes, office spaces, and retail spaces—to paint a much clearer picture of the health and stability of the local economy at the micro level. This also helps you forecast supply and demand. Building permits help you see growth in advance because they are pulled before building begins.
2. *Employment.* Where there is employment, the need for affordable housing is sure to follow. Over time, this can be a key indicator of who your target demographic is. A strong demand for housing can positively impact your occupancy rates and give you the ability to increase your rents steadily over time, which, in turn, increases the value of your property.
3. *Average household size.* This is used to help determine the proper unit mix. If you learn that the average size is 3.7 persons per household, then pursuing a building with a mix of studio and one-bedroom apartments won't work.
4. *Demographics.* Demographics determine who will rent from you. This information gives you the age, gender, and income level of a group of people, and it also helps to give a picture of who the prospective tenant will be. When searching for demographics, also note the total population of the area and how fast it is growing. Growth means more people looking for a place to live.

5. *Psychographics.* Psychographics dictate why someone will rent from the property manager or why they won't. Put differently, demographics tell you who a person is, psychographics tell you what he wants. Knowing who the typical renter is and anticipating his needs in advance—including what amenities he'll want (garages, covered parking, pools, in-unit washers and dryers, walk-in closets, proximity to highways, bus transportation)—will help you focus on the right kind of building for your market and dramatically reduce the likelihood of vacancies.

6. *Mortgage interest rates.* These help to evaluate and determine market cycles. If rates are at an all-time low, more people will be qualifying for mortgages and are therefore less likely to be in the rental market. When the money supply is tight and lenders are cautious and interest rates are high, that's when you're in the best position as a rental property owner. And when rates are low but lending standards are tight for the middle-income demographic, this demographic will typically be forced to rent.

7. *Rental market rates.* A survey is a vital tool that will identify the base rental rates in the area according to the respective unit size. Looking at the rental rate history in an area helps you determine where rents are currently and where they will be in the future. Sophisticated investors buy property based not only on where rents are now but also on where they are headed. The rental rate history gives you the ability to forecast into the future. There are no crystal balls, but understanding how key economic indicators affect rental rates in your targeted area will help to forecast the conditions that will help maximize results.

8. *Occupancy rates.* This is the percentage of currently rented units. This helps you forecast how many vacant units to average in your numbers so that your financial calculations are based on accurate vacancy estimates. If you are significantly off in this estimate, it can have a serious negative impact on your expected cash flow.

For current resources to help you obtain SEOTA information, visit www.landlordacademy .com.

How I Personally Use the SEOTA Information to Help Identify Opportunities in Advance

You now understand how important it is to look to the future trends that will determine whether an area is worth investing in. But now that you know what to include in your SEOTA report, and where to look for it, what exactly do you do with this information? It is, after all, a lot of data to take in and evaluate. We are going to use some hypothetical research statistics to reveal the process of evaluating key indicators of population growth, which will help you better understand how the data is used.

Let's say that you have done some initial due diligence work to determine that a place is worth investigating. For example, let's say you're intrigued by the growth rate of the middle-class demographic in Tampa, Florida, but you notice that the population growth is not supported by growth in wages. You also notice that along with growth in the middle-income population, there are positive periodic decreases in the unemployment rates in the area. Keep in mind your SEOTA is helping to identify trends; there must be no less than three months' worth of supporting historical data before you use the word *trend*.

Let's assume we have historical data supporting our findings. We can also see that new construction is up for the Class A property type; although this is always good to know, as we are an investment group whose focus is on affordable housing, our time is not spent on evaluating the new construction of Class A property types or the absorption rates of their vacant units. We know that our demographic is not looking on Zillow for these types of properties, as our prospective tenant demographic is priced out of this type of rental property. Our data also reveals a slight decline in home ownership, spurred on by the Federal Reserve increasing interest rates.

We begin to forecast the impact of the SEOTA indicators on our prospective tenant's demographic class (middle income) and we forecast an affordable housing shortage. A peaking economy will raise interest rates, along with increasing debt. The opportunity for investing in rental property should be clear: an investor will look to offer the market supply to meet the anticipated demand for affordable housing. Investors who are looking at this opportunity will look to midsized apartment projects to fill the void, mostly Class B and C garden style. You will learn more about asset classes in Step 2. Some will look to single-family homes as well to fill the need for affordable housing.

Additional Tips for Evaluating Potential Opportunities for Rental Property

We also have to consider what kinds of units will best suit this future market. By doing our SEOTA due diligence, we can make educated, strategic decisions. We won't be reactive; we will instead be proactive. I have learned over the years that those who are proactive tend to find the most success.

Additional factors can also be important to middle-income families. Remember, you have to think like your prospective tenants, and their needs may be different from your needs. Some of these needs may be:

- Close to highways and public transportation (bus lines, subways, etc.)
- Close to retail and shopping
- Close to large employment centers

Here is a checklist you can use as you begin your evaluation of a target area. I like to have property managers organize their SEOTA information into an app. That will allow for video recording, pictures, and text. I'm currently using an app called Notability for my iPhone and iPad. I use this checklist as a table of contents that also serves as a quick summary of the SEOTA details on the app.

SEOTA CHECKLIST

Target Area: _____

Preparation Date: _____

1. **Basic Area Information & Map**
2. **Building Permits (i.e., single-family, multifamily, commercial)**
   # of Single-Family _____   # of Multifamily _____   # of Commercial _____
3. **Employment**
   Largest Employment Class _____   Average Income _____
   Second Employment Class _____   Average Income _____
   Has employment been stable in the local area? _____
   Any impact from national employment anticipated? _____
   Comments: _____
4. **Average Household Size & Income**
   Average Household Size _____   Average Household Income _____
5. **Demographics & Psychographics**
   Annual Median Income: _____
   Summary/Comments: _____
6. **Mortgage Interest Rates**
   Current Mortgage Interest Rates: _____
7. **Market Survey**
   Studio Average Rent: _____
   1-Bedroom Average Rent: _____
   2-Bedroom Average Rent: _____
8. **Occupancy Rates**
   Current Average Occupancy Rates _____

Buildings Don't Pay Rent, People Do!

Most real estate books talk only about the building, how to evaluate it, buy it, and turn a profit on it. I believe this is backward thinking. In my experience, the building is the second part of the equation. You should first turn your focus to the people who will rent your property, and learn what the renters in your target area actually want, based on demographic and psychographic data. Once you have that information, you can then find a building that fits those needs. When you learn to anticipate your target demographic's needs in advance, you will be less likely to find yourself with a vacant rental unit.

STEP 2: KNOW YOUR ASSET CLASSES

The second step in the SEOTA process is understanding the different types of property asset classes and how these differences impact operations for the property manager and investor. Most real estate books teach the reader to look for the investment property. All they focus on is the building itself, but the truth is that in the time that I have been in this industry, bricks and mortar have never paid me rent. *People pay the rent.* Many investors and property managers fail to understand this simple fact, and that is why they have trouble filling vacancies on their rental property and their cash flow suffers. I want you to think about rental properties in the way a big business like Walmart thinks about their customers. You have customers, just like Walmart does. Yours are your tenants.

In addition to understanding the prospective tenants you plan to attract, you must also understand the types of properties you can invest in. And, ultimately, that decision will play a large role in determining who your future tenants are.

Real estate books and media outlets tend to make very general statements about real estate markets and their current economic conditions. Statements like "Vacancy rates are extremely high" or "Rental rates are softening" are confusing because they are too general and don't apply to any specific segment of the market. The key for the real estate investor is to drill down to the specific segment of the market the individuals are speaking about, and to determine whether it applies to the class of property they own.

There are several different classes of properties that a real estate investor can own. Each one has its own opportunities and challenges. These classes are:

1. Class A and Class B
2. Class C
3. Class D

Let's take a closer look at them:

1. *Class A and Class B:* These luxury and semi-luxury properties are typically located in high-end areas. These classes are typically associated with luxury condos, luxury rentals, high-end single-family homes, or high-end luxury multifamily buildings. The demographics and psychographics of tenants in these classes will be completely different from the demographic and psychographic profiles of middle- and low-income tenants. What affects the rich does not affect the middle- and low-income tenant, so you have to be very conscientious when making investment decisions.

   Typically, these properties are going to be priced at market or over market. As a result, the investor has to understand that he is not necessarily buying for high returns, but for the anticipation of appreciation of assets over time. A break-even cash flow and above-modest appreciation typically makes paying at market or slightly over market more justifiable, depending on the forecast conditions. This is a costly but sound investment when you consider that high-end properties typically are more stable when it comes to income-producing assets. Delinquencies as well as costly turnovers can railroad the net operating income on other asset classes fairly quickly, making it difficult to achieve positive cash flow, even on properties that were priced at below-market value. This is generally not the case for Class A and B properties.

2. *Class C:* Class C properties typically cater to the middle-income demographic. When investing in Class C properties the investor again must pay attention to the demographics and psychographics of the tenants. Understanding employment factors is key in this segment because middle income is considered to be stable but fixed, meaning that the household income typically grows at a moderate pace, depending on various economic cycles. That is why it is very important for you to do your historical due diligence before investing in this asset class. When you understand this demographic's employment conditions and short- and long-term forecast, it makes investing in this product type a little easier. Personally, I like this asset class because tenants are typically more likely to be long-term renters, especially with today's economic conditions, and have access to capital, which means they can keep up with rent payments. However, transition and turnover will occur more often than with high-end properties, and issues like delinquencies increase a bit more in this asset class as well.

3. *Class D:* One reason that many investors—especially those who are just starting out—are attracted to this asset class is that the acquisition price is lower. The generally low price of Class D properties allows for individuals with limited access to capital to participate in real estate investing and typically make their first purchase. On its own, that is good reason to invest in some of these properties in low-income, sometimes blighted, neighborhoods. But keep in mind that this particular demographic and asset type is extremely volatile. The tenants who typically rent these properties are at or near the poverty line, so their income and their ability to generate consistent income is unpredictable. It's also important to remember that when there are economic downturns, the low-income demographic is the first to take a hit. Their wages are the first to be cut and their hours are the first to be slashed. A reduction in hours and wages results in the inability of these individuals to pay rent, resulting in high evictions and a high turnover rate. This ultimately erodes the net operating income and may require the investor to spend his own money to cover the mortgage.

I also know from personal experience that Class D properties require much more involvement from the investor than other classes. Simply put, a small Class D duplex can require the same amount of manpower as a ten-unit Class B apartment building. It is possible to make these properties work for you, but you have to be particularly savvy in property management when dealing with Class D assets.

You may be asking yourself, what if I do not have the cash to invest in a Class C asset? Should I not invest in a Class D? This is a good question, one that I will not answer for you. However, I will offer up my advice through experience with facing this question myself at one point. I chose to invest in the Class D property because I felt confident in my ability to deliver on the property management side. This actually made me more valuable to the investment group, as I was the only one of the group who could handle a more challenging property. If you decide to take on a more challenging property like Class D, then you will need the skill sets. This is where skills pay the bills!

Once You Have Identified Your Area of Opportunity

After a property manager has helped their client identify an area of opportunity, the next step will be to evaluate potential investment deals. This is where most books or self-proclaimed experts start their process. But not us: we do not put the buggy before the horse, we allow the SEOTA process to choose the areas of opportunities based on our solid key indicators. Now the SEOTA process will move its attention to the actual investment properties themselves. This process of evaluating investment opportunities is the fun part for most people, and why not? Most of our reality shows are based on the excitement of the real estate transaction. The only difference is this ain't no reality show: you're dealing with real people's money. And because this is not a reality show, there are no opportunities for a do-over. They say numbers never lie; well, I beg to differ. If you lack the ability to perform the proper due diligence, you can easily be purchasing a potential nightmare. During this process was when I first heard the phrase "inspect what you expect."

Evaluating Rental Property: How to Find the "Value Add"

You will see a lot of opportunities that other investors overlook. Many investors, even successful and sophisticated ones, look at the financial bottom line of a property, which usually provides a calculation called capitalization rate (cap rate), or cash-on-cash return. If the rate isn't high enough for them, they discard the property and move on. However, we are going to look further at what makes up these calculations and see how often diamonds in the rough are overlooked. You may be asking yourself whether there are any other factors that an investor takes into account before deciding to buy a property. And the answer is yes. You may hear the term "value add" used by investors. This simply means that the investor or investors see opportunity; this opportunity may be viewed from a few different perspectives. Let's take a look at a few value-added opportunities that may exist with respect to a particular property:

1. *Potential growth in the area.* This is a unique instance where your SEOTA process turned up information that most property owners do not yet know about, allowing an opportunity for appreciation above most estimates.

2. *Underperforming management at the operational level.* This simply means that the current property manager is not maximizing income and minimizing expenses. (Skilled property managers always properly maintain the property and will always look to increase the rents.) You would be surprised how often this happens, allowing for another investment group to immediately add value to the property as soon as they implement their new property management team. Always remember that value is often determined by the day-to-day operations of the property manager.

3. *Property rehab opportunities.* This can be a "value add" move on the investor's part. I list this with caution, as it typically requires someone on the team to have a keen understanding of the rehab process. Again, this isn't a reality show! You really need to have a handle on the construction process and have a great working relationship with contractors and vendors who will help you achieve the anticipated values you seek. I have personally seen otherwise skillful property managers take on a major rehab project that got off track and then quickly lose credibility.

Understanding How to Skillfully Acquire Rental Property Can Set You Up for Future Ownership Opportunities as an Investor

Understanding how to buy and manage real estate investment property is the single most important skill set you can acquire. No matter what your experience level, it's important to study the information I'm about to cover. This information alone will open the doors to opportunities for you to manage investors' property and learn from the ground up what it takes at the operations level to run and maintain investment properties. If you study well and master these skill sets, you will be on your way to using a property management company as leverage to participate in larger midsized apartment deals.

That's how I got started: I used my property management business as leverage to participate as an owner without putting any of my own money in the investment, knowing that in most cases the jockey is more important than the horse. I substituted money with my skills as a successful property manager.

When an entrepreneur can successfully negotiate 10 percent ownership for a reduction in management fees, in ten deals they have created 100 percent ownership, without putting any of their own money in the deals. You may ask why an owner would want to give up 10 percent ownership. The answer is simple: owners need to have a skillful property manager on board to first secure loans as well as increase the opportunity to secure more capital from other investors. They also like the guarantee that if all hell breaks loose, someone on the ownership team will know how to guide the ship during any and all changes in the market.

Understanding "Value"

It has been said that there are those who know the price of everything but the value of nothing. No two properties are alike; property values are determined not by perceived value but by value based on what is known as an income approach. This simply means that an income property should only be valued based on the income it can produce. Many will attempt to sell you investment property based on what is known as pro forma income, perceived future value. Most of this perceived value comes from estimating higher future rents. And this is where most property managers and their clients who forgo the SEOTA process will begin to make mistakes in determining the investment's true value.

As I stated previously, investment property should only be purchased from an income approach, and for a professional property manager to know true value, they must first know the truth about the property's income and expenses. This next step will teach you the basics of properly advising your clients on how to analyze a property's income and expenses. Early on, I wanted to express to those I would speak to how each investment has its own characteristics that contributed to its value. To make explaining it easier, I began to call the evaluation phase "the DNA phase." When you think of DNA, you think of getting to the core of what makes up the subject you are evaluating. I wanted those on my team to understand that our job was to uncover the investment's current value and its potential future values, building block by building block, leaving nothing to chance. Now, please keep in mind these are the basics to determine investment properties' cash-flow values, but as is always the case, once I mastered the basics, the more sophisticated measures of determining value became much easier to understand. This next section is designed to help you grasp the fundamentals.

STEP 3: EXAMINE THE DNA STRAND OF A PROPERTY

The next thing the investor should evaluate is the financial makeup of the property. The financial DNA of an investment property is the fundamental makeup of a property's financial performance. First, let's learn what the DNA is. Then, I'll teach you how to inspect each component of the DNA to see whether you can make this property produce more than it currently does.

Before we move into the DNA calculation, let's go over asset classes and all the DNA key terms and formulas. Then we'll put these definitions and formulas to work in a practical application.

GPI (Gross Potential Income)

An investor's main source of income is the rents he takes in. As a property manager, this is your main source of income as well, as you will take a percentage of those rents. The GPI is the maximum possible rental income you can collect if all of the units are being rented, and this figure is calculated on an annual basis. To find GPI, add up the rent on each unit and multiply the amount by twelve, to calculate twelve months of collections. As an example, if you manage a duplex with each side renting for $950 a month, you take the total rents you will collect each month ($950 x 2 = $1,900) and multiply that number by twelve ($1,900 x 12) to get an annual total of $22,800. That's your gross potential income of the property.

VAC (Vacancy Loss)

In a perfect world, all of your units would be rented all the time. Unfortunately, that's not always going to be the case, so we have to allow for some vacancies when we are putting together a financial forecast for the property. This is known as **vacancy loss**. We also have to assume that not everyone will pay all the rent all the time. We call this loss of income **collection loss**. The average vacancy rate used by investors is 5 percent. It's more accurate to determine the average vacancy rate in your specific target area, which is a step of your SEOTA. You don't want to be surprised with a higher vacancy rate than you expected. Now, to determine what vacancy loss means to your property evaluation in dollars and cents, take the GPI (the total yearly rent of all units added together) and multiply that figure by your vacancy rate.

$$GPI \times \text{estimated vacancy rate} = VAC \text{ (vacancy loss)}$$

So, continuing with our duplex example, let's assume an average vacancy rate of 5 percent. We would multiply our GPI of $22,800 by .05, which would equal $1,140. This is our expected vacancy loss for the year.

Effective Gross Income (EGI)

$$GPI - VAC = EGI$$

Effective gross income is defined as your total income from possible rents minus VAC and collection loss. Again continuing with our duplex example, our GPI of $22,800 minus our VAC of $1,140 gives us an EGI of $21,660. This is the amount we can expect to collect on the property per year from the rent roll.

OI (Other Income)

Other income (OI) is defined as money received from sources other than rent. Washing machines and dryers, vending machines, parking fees, application fees, and other sources of income are examples. When you add OI to EGI you get gross operating income (GOI).

$$EGI + OI = GOI$$

The GOI is the total amount of cash the property has available to pay expenses.

$$GPI - OE\ (Operating\ Expenses) = NOI\ (Net\ Operating\ Income)$$

Any expense incurred in operating the property is considered an operating expense. Some of these are fixed and others are variable. An example of a fixed operating expense is property taxes. An investor knows in advance what that dollar amount will be. A variable operating expense is something like eviction costs. The investor knows he will pay them, but he doesn't know how often he will have this cost or what the total will be. Typically, a seller will provide an investor with the total operating expenses of the property at the time of sale. However, I always add 3 to 5 percent to their total. You can also have a home inspector or maintenance technician take a look at the expense total and see whether it's in the ballpark of reasonable.

$$GOI - OE = NOI$$

When you take the gross operating income and subtract operating expenses, you get the net operating income. Think of this as the difference between your before-taxes income and your actual take-home pay. NOI is the income remaining after all expenses are paid, except for your mortgage payment. NOI is a key figure in all the calculations of a property's value from here on out.

Net operating income is like blood to the body. Without blood, the body dies. Rents make up 99.9 percent of net operating income, so if you take away rents from the property, the property dies. One of the biggest mistakes I see investors make is taking the NOI of a property at face value. If 99.9 percent of the NOI is made up of rents, doesn't a property's rent schedule warrant a closer look?

You will be amazed at how many properties are underperforming because the rents charged are too low. This is where my background as an apartment complex manager is worth its weight in gold—and where, as a property manager, you can offer the most value to investors.

It's commonplace in the apartment industry to do monthly market rent surveys, in which an investor or property manager calls nearby complexes and gets their rental rates to make sure his are not too high or too low (you can also do this research online, with a tool like Rentometer.com). It seems so easy, but there are always numerous properties for sale for which the rents are not in line with the current market rents.

This is a great tip for you to know as you consult and seek to partner with investors. Many investors will pass right over a deal because the cap rate or cash-on-cash return looks too low. But you, as an educated property manager, know to take a closer look at what makes up all those fancy formulas—and that, my friend, is the rent. Understand what you can charge for rent and you are on your way to understanding the *true* value of a rental property.

RRA (Replacement Reserves Account)

An RRA is intended to be used for replacement costs of items and materials that wear out, such as roofing, boilers, exterior paint, and parking areas.

DS (Debt Service)

Debt Service is better known as your mortgage payment.

$$GPI - VAC + OI = EGI - OE - RR = NOI - DS = BTCF$$

FE, VE, and RR are the operating expenses in the figure below.

When we put this all together, we get **Before Tax Cash Flow (BTCF)**. This is the cash flow the property will produce before considering taxes.

The Da Vinci Code of Rental Investing

After reading about all of these key terms and formulas, I can most certainly understand why you may find yourself scratching your head. It took me a long time to grasp all of these formulas and apply them, so I encourage you to read this more than once to fully grasp all the concepts. To help you, I have created what I call the Da Vinci Code of Rental Investing. This code examines the three most important formulas used by investors, appraisers, and banks to determine a property's value. These formulas are:

$$CAPITALIZATION\ RATE\ (CAP\ RATE) = NOI/Value$$
$$Cash\text{-}on\text{-}Cash\ Return = NOI - Debt\ Service = BTCF/Owner's\ Equity$$
$$DCR = NOI/Annual\ Mortgage\ Payment$$

Capitalization Rate (Cap Rate) = NOI/Value

Cap rates are primarily used to help estimate the value of income properties. The cap rate is a measure of the absolute return on dollars invested. It does not consider the use of borrowed funds (i.e., leverage); it considers only the return on an investment as if you paid all cash for the investment.

For example, if a property has an NOI of $100,000 and the price of the property is $1,000,000, then the cap rate is 10 percent.

Rule of thumb: Typically, the lower the cap, the higher the price of the property.

💡 BRYAN'S TIP 💡

Keep in mind that a cap rate is like those investment opportunities that I saw on my SEOTA map: it's all subjective. A cap rate is calculated using NOI, which is verifiable, but it's divided by value, which is totally debatable. Everyone can have an opinion on value—the bank, the seller, the appraiser, the investor, and you, the property manager.

Cash-On-Cash Return = NOI – Debt Service = BTCF/Owner's Equity

The cash-on-cash return is the ratio of annual before-tax cash flow to the total amount of cash invested, expressed as a percentage. In other words, cash-on-cash return differs from the cap rate when the investor considers that they have used leverage, i.e., have acquired a mortgage. So, simply put, the cap rate is the return on investment when the investor has paid all cash for an investment, while cash-on-cash return factors in the use of borrowed funds. With that said, the investor surely will want the cash-on-cash return to be higher than the cap rate. If the cap rate is higher than the cash-on-cash return, the investor has borrowed money with a negative repayment rate.

The cash-on-cash return formula is extremely important because it allows the investor to determine returns after using other people's money to help purchase the investment. This is why the wise investor chooses real estate. The use of borrowed funds to increase your returns is hard for any other investment vehicle to beat. It's also very important to mention that banks are used as the most common source for obtaining leverage. Accessing that leverage at a favorable rate is highly depended upon by the investors to manage the property. It's one of the single most important aspects of investing, and one that few ever master.

DCR = NOI/Annual Mortgage Payment

The key here is understanding that NOI (net operating income) shows up in all the formulas. Pause for a second . . . and ask yourself what makes up 99 percent of NOI; with most investments, you're correct if you said rent, especially single-family and smaller apartment buildings. Once you fully grasp this information, you will be a valuable resource to real estate investors and you'll be miles ahead of other property managers.

I personally believe that not having a proper understanding of what can affect NOI is where a lot of property managers begin to lose traction when working with investors, especially if the property manager has never owned investment property. A property manager must understand that different types of asset classes can have a dramatic impact on the investment property itself. As a quick example, the same thirty-unit apartment building will have two totally different property values in two different zip codes. This is the effect that different asset classes have on the bottom line. The SEOTA process identified the differences, mostly in the demographics and psychographics. Now you're going to see how they impact the bottom lines of the investments and of the property management business. Keep in mind that where your property is located will have a tremendous impact on your management systems. Here are a few examples where different asset classes will have a dramatically different impact on the day-to-day operating systems:

- *Tenant qualifying criteria:* Every property location has different challenges. This is primarily due to the demographics of the prospective tenants in the rental property's location. Simply put: different wages, different needs. These differences are no small thing to a property manager—knowing the prospective tenants' needs can have a positive or negative impact on the net operating income the property produces.
- *Tenant rules and regulations:* With different tenant demographics you will need different sets of rules. Personally, our property rules and regulations change from property to property. Some of our more challenging properties located in rougher neighborhoods will often require more emphasis on the rule that all tenants living in the unit must be on the lease. This is due mainly to tenants allowing a roommate to live on the property to help cover the expenses. A good idea, but a potential problem for the property manager, as not having all occupants on the lease can open the property manager and owner to liability issues.
- *Unit mix:* Understanding your prospective tenants' needs when it applies to the number of bedrooms and bathrooms is all about demographics. If the average household in your rental property area consists of 4.5 people, you will find it difficult to rent one- or two-bedrooms units.
- *Ability to raise rental rates:* The main challenge is understanding your market; knowing what a tenant will pay for rent based on their income level is key. The main reason you see properties sitting on listing sites like Zillow for more than thirty days is because the landlord or property manager is most likely out of touch with the rental

market. Setting the rents according to the owners' needs rather than the prospective tenants' needs is always a recipe for future problems.

Reflect on this section for a bit, at least until you have mastered the ability to transfer most of these formulas to a spreadsheet to help you streamline your property evaluation process.

How to Perform the Due Diligence on Your Investment Property

Remember, you're looking to justify the asking price and determine the property's true value from an income approach. As a property manager you will need to help advise your investor clients on how to properly evaluate an investment property. You have heard me say before that numbers never lie; well, they may not lie but they most certainly can be manipulated. There is another famous saying: the devil is in the details. A lot of investors and real estate professionals are unaware of what actually make up the details as they pertain to the investment property. Especially when it comes to evaluating more advanced commercial assets such as apartment buildings.

Below, I have provided a checklist that reveals all of the hidden details that must be evaluated by the property manager. This is where the property manager is different from just another real estate salesperson who is looking to complete a sales transaction and move on to the next deal. As a professional property manager you have a tremendous opportunity to display true value to your client by showing that you truly know what it takes to properly evaluate an investment property at the due diligence level. I cannot express enough how important mastering this process is. Knowing without a doubt that you have a strong grasp of the facts will make the difference in your client's ability to achieve the goals set for the investment; and just as important, it will affect your ability to manage the property effectively.

This process will help you determine, line item by line item, the accuracy of key indicators of the investment, such as:

- Property financial data
- Tenant financial data
- Tenant security deposits
- Tenant financial ledgers
- Tenant leases accuracy
- Property rent roll ledgers
- All property expenses, both fixed and variable
- Vendor contracts
- Risk management assessments

Property Evaluation Checklist

- Prepare letter of intent
- Sign off by (date) _____
- Review and sign off by legal team
- Make sure:
  - Due diligence will expire without obligation by buyer
  - Deposit release requires written action
  - Sufficient time is allowed for due diligence
  - Sufficient time is allowed for financing
- Preapproval letter from lender
- Deposit goes hard on (date) _____

This section contains the preliminary items that will need to be reviewed before you actually set foot on the property. You will want to make sure the seller has provided you with most, if not all, of the information listed in this section. Having this information will set the tone for obtaining the rest of the items in this checklist.

Purchase Agreement

- Confirm investment commitment date
- Deposit goes hard on (date) _____
- Sufficient time allowed for due diligence
- Sufficient time allowed for due financing
- Deposit release requires written action
- Due diligence will expire without obligation by the buyer
- Review and sign off by legal team
- Review and sign off by (date) _____

During this period, you will want to have all the details about the purchase reviewed. Keep in mind that the purchase price may change if the buyer finds something wrong with the information the seller provided. The key is to find this out before you fully purchase the property.

Financing

- Select lender
- Send preliminary numbers to lender
- Calendar of any dates that were agreed to
- Prepare and send lender package

- Send all lender-required documents to appropriate personnel (e.g., rent rolls, leases, and P&L statements for the past three to four months)
- Agree to and verify closing date and funding date

At this time, you will want to have selected your lender. You will want to make sure you share all the due-diligence information with the lender. Keeping the lender in the loop will help set a positive tone. Remember, having the lender's trust that you know how to evaluate and operate the investment will make the difference in getting the deal closed.

Comparable Properties

- Complete economic rent comps
- Complete at least three market surveys along with shopping the target area sales comps
- Complete economic sales comps
- Tour sales comps of other like properties
- Check accuracy of market rents with third-party sources (e.g., locator services)

Remember, everything revolves around value. Investment property value is often determined by net operating income, and 99 percent of NOI is often made up of rent. So verifying that your rental rates are accurate for your current rents and pro-forma rents will ensure you have the correct assumption about the property's value.

Market Survey Rental Income Check

- Obtain the most current rent roll
- Verify rent roll totals by running a tape
- Verify current rents in place match up with the deal sheet
- Verify market rents on the street match up with the deal sheet
- Verify rents match up with the operating statements

Net operating income is like blood to the body; if you negatively affect the blood flow, the body will have major issues. The same applies with cash flow and the investment property. Negatively affect cash flow with inaccurate numbers as it applies to the property and you will not have an accurate picture of the property's value based on the income.

Lease Audit Completed

- Check leases to make sure they match up with rent rolls provided
- Check deposits to make sure they match up with rent rolls and leases

- Check all move-out dates to make sure they match up with rent rolls
- Check tenant correspondence with current management and ownership
- Check leases for any side deals or concessions with tenants
- Check the cash deposits against the collected rents

You hear the term "rent roll" used a lot in this section, so let's quickly define what a rent roll is. Rent rolls for rental property contain the full name of the tenant, when they moved in, when they will move out, their rent amount, any balances or credits on their rental ledger, and the amount of security deposit paid. This information is typically provided by the seller in the form of a report generated by property management software.

Escrow Accounts

- Check tenants' security deposits against owner's escrow account holding deposits
- Open escrow account for security deposits to be transferred before or at closing
- Check owner's reserves for replacement account

You will want to make sure that the bank statement matches what your rent roll says you have in total security deposits paid by the tenants. Any discrepancies that you overlook can come back to haunt you after you become the owner.

Rent Growth Forecast and Market Survey

- Verify by third-party research
- Check reliable sources for rent growth
- Check to make sure that rent growth percent is used in financial projections for each year

The goal is to maximize income and minimize expenses with rental property. This is very difficult if the ownership and property manager do not include future rent growth.

Vacancy

- Check historic vacancy for the past three years
- Calculate financial projections vacancy based on market survey info

Understanding your market's vacancy is key to understanding the property's potential loss income due to vacancy. When evaluating the investment property, you will always want to use accurate numbers to determine an accurate value of the property. I encourage you to go back and reread the DNA of a real estate investment property to ensure you understand this section. Keep in mind, you are not trying to remember the formulas—you are trying to understand them. Remembering works when attempting to pass a test. However, understanding something will keep you out of trouble.

Bad Debt

- Check history of bad debt
- Check to see if bad debt is included in cash flows

You will want to include any of the properties' bad debt to ensure accuracy in the seller's numbers. Remember, we are not paying for any of the seller's current operating mistakes.

Other Income

- Receive reports showing other income generated by property
- Review other income for accuracy*

Note: Do not evaluate nonrecurring items; do not evaluate forfeited deposits

Laundry Contracts

- Check to see whom they are with
- Check to see last time renewed
- Check to see when they expire
- Check what the vendor and landlord splits are

Operating Expenses

- Obtain copies of all service contracts from seller
- Review and make sure cancelable in thirty days
- Obtain list copies of all insurance claims for past year from seller
- Obtain list of pending litigation (if any)
- Obtain a list of any government notices or code informant claims
- Verify number of office personnel and payroll

This is where the rubber meets the road most times. You will often find that what the seller reports may not be accurate with what you will be paying the day you take over the property. Trust, but verify . . .

Advertisement Cost

- Review all advertising contracts
- Make sure all contracts are cancelable in thirty days or less upon purchase

General and Administration Cost

- Review equipment lease
- Verify all office leases are cancelable within thirty days
- Review supply list and pricing
- Review legal expenses (e.g., evictions)
- Review business permits and the renewal date of each
- Review pool permits
- Review janitorial costs

Management Fee Costs

- Select property management company, if you are outsourcing management
- Agree to the fee you will pay company or, if you are managing yourself, determine the fee you will pay yourself and add to financial projections
- Review pest control cost
- Review historical data for expenses
- Examine any unusual items or indication of recurring items
- Include above items in financial projections

Landscape Cost

- Review historical costs
- Review general condition of existing landscape
- Check condition of irrigation system, clocks, and timers
- Budget fully for landscape improvements

Apartment Turnover Costs

- Check historical turnover rate
- Check historical turnover cost per rental unit
- Factor turnover rate into operating costs
- Factor turnover costs per unit, including any unusual turnover expenditures (e.g., wallpaper, stoves)
- Check maintenance checklist to see what items need to be budgeted for

Repair and Maintenance Cost

- Review maintenance checklist
- Check historical maintenance costs
- Review any unusual items that showed up on the maintenance checklist
- Pull out nonrecurring capitalized items
- Evaluate any work orders unit by unit (should show up on maintenance checklist)

Utilities

- Evaluate historical cost for service providers:
  - Water/Sewer
  - Gas
  - Electricity
  - Trash
  - Other
- Speak personally with utility providers re: forecasted rate increases (include in financial projections)

Property Tax and Insurance

- Recalculate property tax based on sales price
- Get insurance bids
- Include new bid in financial projections
- Receive personal property insurance quote
- Obtain hurricane insurance (if needed)
- Include all new quotes in financial projections

Reserves

- Check historical capital expenditures
- Evaluate recurring items of concern
- Create adequate reserves amounts

You will want to make sure that there is an accurate amount of reserves on hand at the property. If not, you will want to use this as a negotiating tool.

Third-Party Due Diligence

- Perform physical inspection
- Complete maintenance check on each unit performed and report reviewed*

Note: Use Subject Property Inspection Checklist (Form 6)

Final Approval Checklist

- Match executive summary with deal summary
- Complete financial review by accounting
- Complete rent-growth assumptions; have them cross-referenced and supported; then sign off on them
- Review refinance option for accuracy
- Review exit strategy tax adjustment
- Check deferred maintenance numbers for accuracy
- Review annual return

Closing–Deal Details

- Check that the closing rent roll was received and approved
- Check tax calculation
- Confirm purchase price on statement is correct
- Confirm seller credits on statement are in order
- Confirm payment of closing cost consistent with contract
- Check to see if financing amount is correct
- Check payment for points
- Check other finance cost and approve
- Check legal costs and approve
- Verify total cash due from buyer

The Five Phases of Real Estate Investing

If I had to sum up all I have learned over the past decade or so—during which time I have been consulting, teaching, investing, and managing—I would break down all the knowledge I have acquired into five phases.

Most of the real estate experts I've met are pros in their specific field, but limited when it comes to the full real estate spectrum. And after working in the real estate industry for more than twenty years, I know exactly how this happens. In general, most books and courses that teach real estate investing highlight just one or two phases of the investment process, but there have been very few that have been written about all five phases of real estate. As a result, even the brightest real estate professionals are launching their businesses and careers with a limited knowledge base. That changes now.

The five phases of real estate are as follows:

1. Acquisition
2. Implementation
3. Stabilization
4. Growth
5. Exit strategy

In my experience, the typical real estate investor is someone who does not have an affinity for any one form of investment. They may be interested in multifamily apartment buildings or single-family rentals, or have an interest in commercial developments like office buildings or warehouses. Maybe they've also considered flipping homes. In any case, this investor is typically very skillful on the acquisition side. He knows how to find the best deals and negotiate the best prices.

The most successful real estate investors and entrepreneurs truly understand how to navigate all five phases, from purchasing, managing, and stabilizing properties to facilitating dramatic growth before executing a sound exit strategy. As a property manager, it is critical that you also learn how to navigate each of these phases, because when you do, you can generate a volatile-proof income that will remain stable regardless of the current economic cycle.

As I go into detail about each of these phases, I want you to pay careful attention to the ways each phase complements the others and how making a mistake in one phase can drastically impact another. For example, if an investor overspends on a property or makes another mistake during the acquisition phase, it is going to be much more difficult to stabilize the property and achieve growth. And if an investor makes a wise purchase but then mismanages the property (e.g., by not hiring an experienced property management firm that can implement the proper systems), he will sabotage his stabilization phase, ultimately hurting his ability to enter the growth phase.

Let's take a closer look at each phase individually.

1. **Acquisition.** The purchase phase of an investment property is one of the most important phases, as it determines how successfully the investor will be able to navigate the other four phases. This phase is all about financial management, and many of the key points to remember were discussed in the SEOTA description earlier in this chapter.
2. **Implementation.** In this phase, the primary responsibility of the investment shifts from the investor to the property manager/landlord, and the property manager's

main goal is to implement the proper systems that will make managing the property as seamless as possible.

Operating systems: Operating systems involve identifying the work that needs to be done and then determining the most efficient and effective way to perform that work both consistently and profitably. Please note that unless a system is documented, it cannot be repeated properly. It is possible to have a system that has developed over time and works well because the landlord or property manager has been doing it that way over time. However, if that process is not written down in detail, that property manager cannot expect to achieve consistent results, namely because he cannot replicate his efforts with other team members. When you own or manage rental property, it is critically important to document systems and remain consistent in their implementation for insurance purposes and legal protection.

Technology systems: While documentation and consistency are the foundation for any business, it can be a cumbersome process. The good news is that both can be achieved by using a combination of property management software and apps. Over the past ten years, these technological advances have allowed a single property manager or landlord to reduce their workload by more than 80 percent. Good property management software should allow you to:

- post tenants' rents to their ledger and check payment history
- generate a work order for a rental and check its progress
- add charges to the tenant ledger
- generate reports, including delinquency, rent rolls, and tenant profit and loss statements
- recognize the difference between single-family, vacation rentals, and apartment buildings
- manage multiple rentals for multiple offers from multiple devices
- support multiple users
- allow the user to post listings to multiple social media and rental platforms

3. **Stabilization.** Stabilization occurs after the proper management systems have been implemented and a landlord or property manager is ready to adequately address the property's income and expenses. In order to accomplish stabilization, the property manager needs to control several key components:

- *Occupancies:* Occupancies are primarily controlled by having a strong grasp on your prospect and putting in the necessary legwork during the strategic evaluation of the target area, which will ultimately help you to have a better understanding of your property's core demographic. Understanding the demographic will then help you control occupancy rates because you will understand the types of units your demographic is looking to rent and how much they are able/willing to pay for them.

- *Rental rates:* Understanding where to place your rental rate is a skill that is highly overlooked by many landlords and property managers. Again, the SEOTA analysis should help you to quickly determine where you need to set your rental rates, thanks to the clear picture of your prospects and their demographic/psychographic profile. Additionally, you should also consider age of the property, overall condition/maintenance of the property, and location of the property.
- *Turnovers:* Losing a tenant, for any extended time, will have a negative impact on future cash flow. This is magnified with single-family units, as single-family properties have only one source of income. Think of it like this: If Owner A has a single-family rental home and he has a vacancy, he has a 100 percent vacancy rate. But if Owner B owns a duplex rental and she also has one vacancy, her vacancy rate is still just 50 percent. Owner B reduced her risk by 50 percent by owning just one more unit, and benefited by having both rentals located in the same place, making them easier to manage.

Ultimately, by owning just one more unit, Owner B benefits from the economy of scale that accelerates rental return. For further illustration of this concept, I want you to think back to the game Monopoly. This game taught us that five green houses would equal a greater cash flow than one red hotel. An investor will want to start with a single-family home, but he would eventually look to move the cash flow into a greater-producing income property that benefits from larger scale. The smart investor with the red hotel also benefits from the ability to manage the assets on a single site, versus having five single-family homes spread over a given geographical area.

Delinquencies: Delinquencies can be drastically reduced by understanding your prospective tenant in advance. Again, I cannot stress enough the importance of a thorough SEOTA evaluation. This due diligence process will help you gain a strong grasp of your prospective tenant, and when a landlord or property manager truly understands his prospects, he can begin to set qualifying criteria that will help eliminate high delinquencies, turnovers, and the high cost of evictions.

Maintenance budgets: When performing your due diligence process and evaluating the rental units, have an inspector/maintenance technician walk through several rental units with you. This process allows you to understand the overall condition of the rental unit to help set the true value of the rental property and allows you to understand future cash flows by forecasting maintenance issues.

4. **Growth.** In the growth phase, the property manager/landlord is focused on maximizing the income of the property and minimizing the expenses. Maximizing the income is accomplished by increasing the net operating income of the property while minimizing the expenses through careful budgeting. Both facets of the equation will change constantly and require maintenance. But once you have successfully increased the income-generating capabilities of the property, you have essentially increased the value of the rental asset. Now you can prepare yourself (and/or your investor) for the final phase.

5. **Exit strategy.** The final stage of real estate investing occurs when the investor determines that he has reached his desired return on investment. Once this phase has been realized, he can either sell the property, reposition the returns in a greater investment, or cash out.

As I mentioned, by gaining a thorough understanding of the five phases of real estate investing, you will be able to walk into any property and know how to turn it into a profitable investment. That knowledge, coupled with your knowledge of the SEOTA analysis and rental asset classes, will take your property management business to new heights.

As you continue reading this book, you will learn many specific business-building strategies, from how to market your services to how to find and hire the right attorney. But none of that matters if you don't have this fundamental understanding of real estate investment. This is your foundation. Reread this chapter as often as necessary.

THREE

DEVELOPING YOUR FOUNDATION

Creating a business plan and setting up a solid corporate structure

It is important that you go into this with a proper mind-set. Play devil's advocate, and question the assumptions you are making. Arrive at the most realistic set of circumstances. Understand your skill sets and experience as well as your limitations and deficiencies. There are different skills and abilities required for each of the many different hats a property manager has to wear.

From a real estate agent's perspective, most get involved in real estate only understanding one specific part of the industry, typically the sales part. Most real estate professionals get thrust into the real estate business without proper preparation or skills. The process of obtaining the required licensing includes education that prepares you to take and pass a test. However, this process falls short of giving the students the necessary skill sets for becoming successful entrepreneurs. Being a great real estate agent does not predict a successful transition into being a great property management entrepreneur, because the latter requires a different set of skills. Naturally, starting any new role and company will involve doing things that you don't have experience with. Understand what you need to know that you don't already and find a way to fill the void.

I am going to teach you how to transition from being great at your real estate niche to being a successful business owner.

CREATING A BUSINESS PLAN

Right now there are a lot of great ideas running through your head. It is vital these ideas be put down in writing to organize them and to help you understand how the pieces work together and flow. The following bullet points are important topics to think about when developing your business plan. Every person and their business plan will be different. The steps you start on will be different. You will restructure and rewrite things after you develop more topics. This list is not necessarily in chronological order. Your completed business plan, which you will be giving to people for review, should be in the standard order, starting with executive summary, then mission statement, management summary, and so on. Your business plan is your creation and should be done in your own way. It is important to have other people look at your business plan to critique it. At the end of this chapter, I'll share with you a sample business plan. But for now, let's examine the table of contents that makes up a traditional property management business plan.

Business Plan Table of Contents

- Executive summary
- Mission statement
- Operating summary
- Target customers
- Company goals
- Keys to success
- Financials
  - Ownership
  - Expense summary
  - Revenue forecast
- Services
- Marketing
  - Overview
  - Segmentation
  - Size and growth
  - Trends
  - Strategy
- Business operations
  - Policies and procedures
  - Personnel requirements
  - Legal
  - Competition
  - SWOT analysis
  - Performance review

Here's a brief explanation of each of the components of your business plan:

- *Executive summary:* Defines your property management company's purpose. Who you are and what you do. The "why" is your company's purpose. The "why" will keep you in the pursuit of excellence. The "what" is your company's vision, helping you to realize what your purpose looks like. The "how" is the process of putting it all together to accomplish your "why" and your "what" (purpose and vision).

- *Mission statement:* Your USP (unique sales proposition).
- *Operating summary:* How does your company operate? Hours, physical location, virtual technology applications.
- *Target customers:* Who are your prospective clients? How does your company meet their needs?
- *Company goals:* Benchmarks to measure achievement within a specified period of time.
- *Keys to success:* The strategy that you will use to achieve your goals.
- *Financials*

  - *Ownership:* Defines who the owners are and how the profits are distributed.
  - *Expense summary:* Evaluates the potential and likely expenses so you are adequately prepared financially.
  - *Revenue forecast:* Break-even analysis and cash-flow analysis need to be completed. Important to understand when and how much your company will have to operate on. Create financial projections for the different sources of revenue.

- *Services:* What services does your company provide?
- *Marketing*

  - *Overview:* An understanding of the demographics (who) and psychographics (why) of your market allows you to anticipate opportunities.
  - *Segmentation:* What are the segments of your market?
  - *Size and growth:* How many customers are there? How many will be there in the future?
  - *Trends:* What outside influences are there on the market? Consider the economy, climate, technology, traditions. How do they change your market?
  - *Strategy:* How do you reach your target clients? Website, social media, blogging, hosting educational events. An understanding of KPIs in conjunction with implementation of a CRM (customer relations management) will help guarantee success with these strategies.

- *Business operations*
  - *Policies and procedures:* What systems does your company use to operate? What are the operating procedures? How do you service your customers? How is the service measured?

- *Personnel requirements:* Who will work for your company? What is the goal of the positions they fill? Make sure you understand that the people who represent your company need to fit the company culture laid out in your executive summary. Are they salaried employees, independent contractors, outside vendors? What is the on-boarding process? What is their career path? How are they compensated? What training and education do they receive?
- *Legal:* Creating your corporation, determining proper licensing requirements (state-specific), obtaining your real estate/broker's license and business license
- *Competition:* What are other competing property management businesses doing to obtain clients? What are they doing well and what are they doing not so well? And how can you compete?
- *SWOT analysis:* An evaluation of the internal strengths and weaknesses, as well as external opportunities and threats.
- *Performance review:* How to track and measure performance and relate it to success. This will help improve efficiency.

If you've started another business in the past, some of this will look familiar to you, as many of these initial steps apply to businesses in any industry. There will also be real estate–specific tasks that you must complete before moving on to the next step. Follow these steps and you will morph from a real estate wannapreneur into a full-fledged real estate entrepreneur.

Step 1: Get licensed.

Each state varies on licensing requirements for property managers, but most require a real estate broker license and/or a property management license. If you can afford it, I would actually recommend that you get both certifications. In addition to fulfilling the necessary requirements, the additional certification will prove to your insurance company that you are knowledgeable about the business and committed to staying abreast of industry best practices, which will likely reduce your premiums.

Step 2: Set up a corporate entity to operate your property management business from.

Understanding how to create the best entity structure for your business will involve conversations with key professionals including accountants and attorneys. You will want to make sure they have a very strong grasp of real estate. One piece of advice that I will share personally with you is, no matter what entity you choose to set up your real estate business, to provide the protections you seek, you will need these things to be considered a business by the judge and an insurer:

1. Business plan
2. Operations manual for the day-to-day functions of operating the business
3. Up-to-date training and education, certificates of course completions and industry designations

Because of the extreme sensitivity of this subject, and its level of importance as the foundation of your vision, we have dedicated an entire section to this subject matter, as well as enlisted the help of a well-seasoned attorney to help guide you.

Step 3: Create the operating agreement.

It is important to set up an operating agreement in the early stages of your company. It spells out the rules of the game. How and when money is to be spent, what contributions are made and required. People's memories, emotions, life circumstances, and business successes or failures all vary. Things when times are good are different from when times are bad. If you are thinking, "Oh, this can't happen to me, so and so would never do that to me," you need to seriously reconsider. It's not as much a matter of *if*, it is a matter of *when* problems will arise. Understand the reasons contracts exist and when they are used.

Step 4: Set up your screening process.

I formed a partnership with TransUnion to create an ideal system for tenant screening. We are now able to remove much of the risk involved in the screening process. After creating the qualifying criteria and inputting them into the TransUnion system, tenants then fill out their information and TransUnion approves or rejects the applicant based on those set criteria. If you do not set up your tenant screening process properly, you expose yourself to discrimination lawsuits. If sued, the creditor will attack the integrity of the corporation, trying to prove you do not or have not maintained or operated the corporation properly. They have many avenues to pursue to prove either of these two claims. If they succeed, it will be like a series of dominos falling. The first will be the insurance coverage you thought you had for your business once they prove you do not have a business. The creditor will look to come after you personally, holding you personally liable. Your insurance company will most likely have informed you they insured your business and not you personally. Basically, what I'm saying is, if the creditor can prove that you don't have a business, then according to your insurance policy you don't have insurance. If you don't have an insurance policy, you don't have coverage to protect you and your family. You can help prevent this disaster from happening by having a clearly defined screening process and qualifying criteria.

Step 5: Set up your property management systems.

Remember you are now dealing with other people's investments, and they will need detailed reporting from you on financial matters. Systems for bookkeeping, document management, customer relations. Property management software and CRM software can do a lot of the heavy lifting for you and help keep you in compliance and your customer satisfaction high.

Step 6: Purchase business insurance.

Property managers wear many different hats while performing their day-to-day operations. In addition to overseeing the maintenance and overall welfare of the properties, they must fulfill duties as:

- Leasing agents
- Real estate agents
- Appraisers
- Construction managers
- Consultants

To successfully perform these operations, a property manager must be knowledgeable and up-to-date with property values, landlord-tenant law, tax regulations, and proper procedures when dealing with law enforcement. Due to the many detail-oriented responsibilities, errors are bound to occur. Whether it's entering the wrong information on the lease agreement or any number of other scenarios that involve the day-to-day operations of property management, these instances can lead to lawsuits.

Without proper insurance, these errors and omissions can be financially overwhelming. Start-up costs for a new property management company are not high; however, your insurance cost makes up a big part of the start-up costs. It is important that this step be taken very seriously and that you make sure to obtain whatever insurance is necessary for your company.

COMMON MISCONCEPTIONS ABOUT INSURANCE COVERAGE

Common misconceptions that property managers have about insurance coverage include the belief that their commercial general liability policies provide coverage against error or omissions, as previously mentioned, or negligence. The general liability policy only covers property damage and personal and bodily injury, as well as advertising injury.

To protect themselves from claims dealing with issues such as fair housing, negligence, misrepresentation, and inaccurate advice, property managers must turn to professional liability insurance also known as errors and omissions, or E&O. This insurance is designed to protect against errors, omissions, and negligence, but typically does not protect against nonfinancial losses.

E&O insurance typically has a claim limit and an annual limit. Understanding your portfolio and scope of work projected when speaking with an insurance professional will be important in making sure you are not over- or underinsuring yourself.

Another aspect of insurance that is often overlooked by property managers is their vendors. It is important that the property management company mitigate their exposure by requiring and verifying that vendors' policies are current. You should have vendor contracts pertaining to the scope of work as well as a vendor/broker agreement detailing liability, required licensing, and insurance.

It is a good idea that the property manager is also well versed in what renter's insurance as well as homeowner's policies their prospective property owners will need and have.

Now is a great time to consider how your real estate investment operations work, and whether you are properly protected in the event things go wrong. Do you purchase properties and rent to individual tenants? Invest in properties that are rented out to businesses? Flip homes? Do you work as a part of an investment group? All real estate investors, regardless of the investment model, should weigh insurance considerations before expanding further into the market.

Investment in commercial property maintains many of the same risks as in the past. Commercial real estate often sees high customer foot traffic, leading to more claims. And as the economy continues its upswing, you may expect consumer spending to increase, in turn leading to more foot traffic and yes, more insurance claims against businesses.

Home flippers and rental property investors will also need to be aware of their liability concerns when renting properties and selling them. Renter and buyer concerns are often great, particularly when costs are rising for both rent and homeownership. Expect both to be demanding in getting the value of their dollar and more likely to take action when issues arise.

WHAT COVERAGES DOES YOUR BUSINESS NEED?

Insurance concerns within the real estate investment market can be mitigated by a number of different insurance products designed to reduce liability and counteract some of the foreseen and statistically predictable claims.

General Liability and Commercial Property

Take general liability and commercial property, for example. Both of these insurance policies are integral for any commercial real estate investment, whether by individuals or investment groups, as they cover many of the primary concerns associated with owning such properties. A general liability policy protects the business against third-party claims, such as those that come from customers who may sustain injuries on the property. Commercial property is an integral addition to this, providing coverage for the property itself, and providing protection should property get damaged.

A business owner's policy (BOP) should be considered if you find both policies suit your needs, as a BOP carries the benefits of both general liability and commercial property, while adding in elements of business interruption insurance that can help you hedge your bets should something occur that results in an inability to draw rental income, or, in the case of a house flip, an inability to sell the property.

You may have also heard of property owners liability coverage, which is often included within a general liability policy. This coverage is designed to mitigate liability for property owners and especially landlords. The purpose is to help provide coverage for claims related to injuries or property damage that renters or others associate directly with the property owner, and not necessarily the current occupant. This can include claims from current residents charging the property owner for negligence in maintaining the property. While not necessarily a large concern for house flippers, investors who focus on renting to individuals and businesses may see this area as one of major concern.

Commercial property investors also may want to consider a terrorism endorsement. Although liability coverage was limited as a result of the Terrorism Risk Insurance Act, this policy allows your business and your properties to be covered specifically for incidents related to both domestic and international terrorism. While there are limits to how much an insurance company offers in coverage, lack of coverage means that the insurance company will not have to cover losses associated with acts of terrorism at all, despite traditional commercial property coverage.

Workers' Compensation

Workers' compensation requirements will vary depending on where your business is located. Per state laws, your business is required to purchase workers' compensation once your business reaches a certain number of employees. In some states this could be as few as one employee beyond yourself, while in other states it may be five or six employees.

Ignoring workers' compensation coverage is never a good idea, as it can be extremely costly to your business to cover the cost of an incident. For real estate investors who employ their own construction and maintenance crews, this is particularly important, as these workers can be at high risk for on-the-job injuries. Lack of coverage means your business may have to cover lost wages and medical expenses directly. Workers compensation, instead, will free you of that direct cost.

Errors and Omissions (E&O)

If your business model involves investing as a professional service with other people's money, you'll need to be particularly cautious with how you manage that money and the financial decisions you make. E&O claims can quickly arise if a client believes money has been mismanaged and purchases made on their behalf were not properly planned out.

Also consider how scaling will impact the cost of your premiums. As you invest on behalf of greater numbers of parties with greater amounts of money, this may have an impact on your premiums. Nevertheless, as your holdings and investment values increase, working with more parties means you have more individuals who may hold you liable should anything go wrong. Essentially, scaling means your risk increases. Your E&O insurance coverage should increase with those risks.

Rent Guarantee Insurance

A separate product from business interruption insurance, rent guarantee insurance is designed to give your business supplemental income in case a renter fails to pay. This policy will only pay out under certain conditions, but may be particularly necessary for businesses buying investment properties in more volatile markets. For commercial property investments in particular, the type of business that you rent the space to may make it more necessary to purchase this insurance. Some businesses, such as restaurants, fail more frequently and often operate with slim profit margins, resulting in a higher risk for missed payments.

WHAT SHOULD YOU ALWAYS DO (OR NOT DO) WHEN SHOPPING FOR A POLICY?

Getting just the right policy with just the right amount of coverage can be tricky. Particularly when you're navigating policy purchases that provide liability coverage for multiple properties. Here are a few things to consider when conducting policy research.

Consider the Replacement Cost of the Property

This one is extremely important for all types of real estate investors. If the property you're investing in is lost today, what is its value? First you'll need to determine what property should be covered and consider whether you want coverage for the replacement cost or actual cost, as these factors will be specified within your policy. That means looking beyond just the physical structure, but everything inside of it that is a part of that property. Determine which costs are associated with the internal structure, such as wiring and plumbing, and any equipment that exists inside the property as well, such as appliances. All of this can add up, and it's important that you make a full assessment.

Find a Broker with Expertise—Such as CoverWallet

As tempting as it is to try to figure this out alone, it could lead you to pay far more in premiums than you need to or, potentially, result in coverage gaps. CoverWallet is making a name for itself as an insurance market leader by helping clients find the best policies for their particular business. The company is focused on putting more power into the hands of business owners, while shifting the industry toward a more technology-focused way of handling insurance.

Look for the Right Coverage Instead of the Cheaper Price

Yes, it's important to find value in your premium. But consider your real estate coverage the same way you would your personal car insurance policy. You *can* get the bare minimum. Yet when it's actually time to use that insurance (say, you hit a deer on a dark road), you'll find that the minimum coverage can often be lacking. Low premiums are a way to say you're covered, but in reality the policy may not protect your business fully when it comes time to actually utilize the policy.

Instead, opt for policies that make sense in terms of coverage and price. Also consider how much of a loss your company can absorb, versus how much the cost of premiums will impact your business. In most cases, there's a happy medium in there somewhere, although you'll generally need a good broker to help you better understand where that middle ground exists.

Invest in Burglar Alarms, Sprinklers, and Fire Alarms

If you're owning and renting property, you may actually find that such an investment in protection and security equipment will lower your commercial property insurance premiums. Generally speaking, these products will help dissuade burglars and aid in limiting damage done to a property in the case of fire. Insurance companies see value in that, and are typically open and willing to provide more inexpensive insurance premiums if they believe your properties hold less risk.

Check for Adequate Liability Limits on All Policies

Before signing on the dotted line, make sure that your liability limits actually meet your needs, as those limits mean that your insurance company only has to pay out up to a certain amount. This may mean finding liability coverage that mitigates the entire cost of your needs, or limits that cover nearly the entirety of your cost, with an acceptable amount remaining that your business can pay.

CERTIFICATES OF INSURANCE (COIs)

It's hard to express how important COIs are to real estate investors, especially those who rent to individuals and businesses. Certificates of insurance are used to help ensure that your tenants have adequate insurance coverage for themselves, and will help prevent those tenants from pushing liability on to you.

Make sure that all tenants are compliant with all contracts. For individual tenants, this may mean ensuring that they have purchased and are current on their renter's insurance policies. For commercial property investments, this may mean requiring that businesses provide COIs for their own general liability and commercial property insurance policies. Again, this helps to assure protection for your business should losses occur and claims arise.

Property investors in particular need to consider carefully the type of coverage that may be most important to require of vendors, agents, and clients. As it is not always tenants whose claims may come back to you, you need to consider how those who are working on and with your property investments are covered. If you're working with a property management company, for example, what insurance policies do you require of them? If you hire construction contractors to work on an investment property, what policies do they need to have to reduce your liability?

Also consider how you will communicate these requirements to them and develop a method that will help you keep current on their insurance purchases. CoverWallet can help you manage your COIs and maintain compliance for your COI requirements.

In all, purchasing and maintaining proper insurance will help keep your business up and running in case the unexpected happens.

More detailed information on insurance can be found later in the book. Additional information and forms relating to insurance can be found in the resources section of our website.

Step 7: Set up your bank accounts in your company name.

You will need three primary bank accounts:

- An **operating account** where you will deposit rent checks and from which you will pay operating expenses.
- An **escrow account** that you will use to hold the deposit each owner gives you to cover minimal and routine maintenance costs.

- A **security deposit account** that you will use to hold the tenants' security deposits. This should be a noninterest-bearing account and these funds should *not* be commingled with other funds or accounts.

Creating Your Business Corporate Entity Structure and Protecting Yourself Further

Galen M. Hair's real estate clients include some of the most prominent real estate developers in Louisiana and beyond. He is enlisted as "rescue counsel" to save multimillion-dollar real estate deals when they appear to be on the brink of failure. Here he shares his insight:

It is my privilege and honor to provide you with this insight into my corner of the world. The below is intended to be insight and general information only. I am licensed in Florida, Massachusetts, New York, and Louisiana. Everyone's situation is different and each and every one of you would benefit from speaking to an attorney who is geographically local to you.

ENTITIES, STRUCTURE, AND CONTRACTS. OH MY!

When you start any business, it is hard to think about anything but keeping the lights on. In that way, starting a law firm is similar to becoming a real estate developer. Focusing on making money today just isn't enough. Stop and let that sink in. In today's world one mistake can undo years of hard work. When people ask me what I do, I often tell them I am in the business of risk management. I have watched large businesses with millions of dollars in assets fail because of one little mistake or one document that is slightly out of order. Similarly, I have seen shrewd businesspeople with legally sound corporate structures survive blunder after blunder.

Several years ago my phone rang unexpectedly. It was a colleague of mine from law school and he had a problem. He had a client sitting in his office who was under full-scale attack. The client's assets were being systematically stripped from him property by property, dollar after dollar. It was clear that his adversary intended nothing short of complete and utter decimation. This quite wealthy gentleman suddenly was seen as a "debtor." Frankly, it was too late. It was no longer about winning the fight—it was about slowing (not stopping) the bleeding. Why did this happen? This happened because this individual did not get a proper contract signed when he needed it most. The funny thing about handshake deals is that everyone has a different version of the story when a dispute arises.

I could regale you with countless stories about how a bad corporate structure combined with oral agreements places you, your family, and your loved ones at risk. For the sake of this chapter, I ask that you just take my word for it.

You see, as is discussed elsewhere in this book, we live in a litigious world. Look at your television, glance up at the billboards. Attorneys are everywhere, and they want anyone and everyone to file a lawsuit. Who can blame them? They right wrongs and fight injustices. What those television ads and billboards don't tell you is that a little knowledge and legal know-how can go a long way toward protecting you when and if the time comes. The other thing those ads *rarely* tell you is that you usually have to take these steps *in advance*.

I could go on for pages about the different types of lawsuits and causes of action, but I want you to get the most possible out of these precious few pages. Rather than scare you, I would like you to focus on how to protect yourself.

Setting Up a Solid Corporate Structure—It's Not Just for the Wealthy, It's for Everyone

LLCs, C corps, S corps, sole proprietorships, partnerships, joint ventures. The list goes on. In fact, it gets even more complicated, because some states have additional types of corporate entities and the laws vary from state to state. We will discuss the most common types of entities and why they may or may not be the right fit for you. In real estate, it is crucial to have the right type of entity. Whether you are building properties, buying properties, selling properties, renovating properties, renting properties, or managing properties, things can go wrong. People can get hurt, deals can fall through, people can default on their monetary obligations. You cannot predict everything that will or could happen, so you have to have an entity in place that protects you.

- **Sole proprietorship.** I want you to think about the phrase "sole proprietorship" for a moment. Great. Now delete it from your memory and never say that phrase again. What I will never tell a client is to start a sole proprietorship and the reasoning is simple. I like my clients, and I want them to succeed. Some people find sole proprietorships tempting. They love to say, "I am the sole proprietor of Big Money Enterprises." Just don't do it. A sole proprietorship means what you probably think it means. You are the only owner. What it doesn't mean is a lot more important, though. Generally, it means you have *zero protection* if something goes wrong. A sole proprietorship is not an LLC, it is not a corporation; in fact, legally speaking it really isn't much of anything. It will not give you an ounce of protection in legal terms. Simply put, there is not much of a reason to ever create a sole proprietorship.
- **Partnership.** A partnership, in a general sense, is just as bad as a sole proprietorship. A partnership in the purest sense is no different from a sole proprietorship other than the fact that there are two or more owners. If your partner makes a mistake, you are also personally responsible. If someone is hurt on a property owned by the partnership, you may have to sell your house to pay for it. In some states, partnerships have some limited protection *between the partners*. This means that a partner could not legally run off with all the money. You could also have a partnership agreement that would govern your rights *between each other*, but would not likely be effective to the rest of the world. As a lawyer, I am thrilled to find an adverse party that is a general partnership because this means I have more pockets

to look to when the time comes to collect. I would rarely recommend a partnership to a client.

Many states support different types of partnerships, including limited partnerships and limited liability partnerships. I am not going to go into those here, because they differ significantly from state to state. While they may be alternatives for you and your business, they are complicated and should never be used without competent legal guidance.

- **Corporation.** You know what a corporation is even if you don't have an ounce of legal knowledge. You know this because they typically are followed by the abbreviation "Inc." or "Corp.," if not the entire word. Corporations are marked as corporations to let the world know that they are a different animal altogether. In many states, corporations are separate "juridical entities." This is another way to say that corporations are basically separate people, legally speaking. This has huge advantages. A corporation has liability for its own acts, but its shareholders (owners) do not usually have liability for the acts of the corporation. This means that if you create a corporation, and maintain it properly (discussed below), your personal assets should be safe. In most states, corporations come in two flavors: C corps and S corps. S corps are by far the more common entity for start-ups because they are easier to manage. C corps are typically used by larger businesses because it is easier to sell stock and bring on investors.

- **Limited liability company (LLC).** LLCs, from a legal standpoint, are pretty young business entities. They have come into favor over the last decade or so, and these days are the most popular entity choice for new (and even large and established) companies. LLCs are popular because they provide asset protection similar to what a corporation provides, offer tax flexibility (you get to choose whether you will be taxed as a S corp or a partnership), and don't have the burdensome corporate formalities that corporations have in some states. When a new client comes in the door, I can typically predict that we will form an LLC for the client. In some states, LLCs are incredibly quick and easy to form. LLCs are owned by "members." LLCs don't have partners, owners, or sole proprietors. They have members. They can be operated by a nonmember, called a manager. Members can operate the entity much like the board of directors of a corporation or even the shareholders of a corporation would. A limited liability company is typically formed with a document called articles of organization. An LLC should also have an operating agreement, which is a formal document that governs how the members should behave in terms of owning and operating the LLC. If you have a multiple-member LLC, your operating agreement is one of the most important legal documents you have. It will tell you what happens when you have a dispute with other members. I cannot tell you how often potential clients do not want to invest the necessary time into fine-tuning their operating agreements, but then show back up at my door (or another lawyer's office) years later with a complicated and expensive legal issue that would have been resolved with this one little document. Additionally, LLCs do not have to have multiple members. You can have a single-member LLC, which will provide far more protection than a sole proprietorship.

- **Other types of entities.** Many states have other types of entities that are available. Some of these may be a good fit for you. Do not simply pick one without first consulting with a lawyer in your area. This is very important. Some of these entities have odd requirements such as a cap on profit! You need to know why these entities are less popular and what you can and cannot do with them.

Separate Roles

Let's say you are buying property, renovating it, renting it out, and then selling it. This sounds like a great business model and it is. What is *not* a good business model? Having the same entity take on each of these roles. You may wish to have one entity that does all the property management, another entity that oversees all renovation, and one or more entities actually holding the properties. This way if something goes wrong at one stage of the process, other properties in other stages are not necessarily hurt. This is a good way to do business, but you will absolutely need a lawyer to help you set this up and show you how it will functionally work.

Corporate Waterfalls—Take It to a Higher Level

I would never recommend that you do this without a lawyer, but one of the best ways to protect yourself as well as your family is to create a corporate waterfall structure. We also call this a corporate fortress. What happens here is that your entity is owned by another entity. Then that entity is owned by another entity and so forth. Within this, a lawyer may create entities to manage one or more of these entities. Then, they may create trusts to hold certain ownership interests in some of these entities. Are you confused yet? If you answered yes, then you understand exactly why this is done. Imagine being a plaintiff. You took the case to trial, you got your judgment, and now it is time to collect. I have created such a spiderweb for you to search through that it may be easier for you to pack up your bags and go home. But, as I said, you should never attempt to implement this strategy without the help of a lawyer and a CPA.

Corporate Formalities and Piercing the Corporate Veil—Walk the Walk

So now you have all these entities, but, frankly, the law doesn't care. It doesn't care if you paid a registration fee to the state. The law cares about whether you actually treat these corporations and LLCs as their own separate legal people. Did you pay your personal electric bill out of the LLC account? Don't! Do you move money around freely with no stated reason for it? Don't. You need to keep good solid business records. Did you make a major decision? Fantastic. Now document it. Keep meeting minutes. Even if you are the only member of your LLC. Have a meeting with yourself and reduce it to writing. Give a lawyer like me a paper trail to follow if I am one day called upon to protect your personal assets. It is of the utmost importance that you can show someone, if called upon to do so, that this entity is not merely your alter ego. This sounds tedious, but just like anything else, if you make it routine, it becomes easy. You do not have to pay a lawyer to prepare meeting minutes for you every time. Your lawyer, though, will be happy to sit down with you and show you what you should be doing and how to do it. This advice, although relatively inexpensive, could save you thousands if not hundreds of thousands of dollars later.

We had a client come to us in the middle of litigation once. His entity had been formed and operated for years before we met him. It was a routine construction matter, and at issue was about a hundred thousand dollars. He had the personal money to pay it, but why would he? The whole point is that his entity was set up to prevent exactly this issue. So what ended up happening? The other side went through all his documents and argued that he wasn't following the appropriate "corporate formalities" and that his company was merely his "alter ego." To be honest, had he done a better job at maintaining these records, we never would have settled the case for the figure we settled it for. But, because that risk was there, the client was forced to settle. This was something this client could have paid a lawyer a few hundred dollars to show him how to do a few years before and it would have saved him a ton of money.

Contracts—the Most Fun You Will Ever Have, Seriously

Contracts are fun. I promise. Not just for lawyers like me, but for everyone. To understand that statement, you have to understand what a contract really is. A contract is a document that governs the rights, obligations, and relationships of the parties to the contract. What does this really mean? It really means a contract is a blank slate. You get to write the book on what you want to do in this contract. What do you want to happen if the contractor doesn't finish on time? What about if the property management company doesn't remit rent in a timely manner? How much notice do you want if there is a problem before the other party can sue you? Do you want a chance to fix the problem first? Do you want attorneys' fees paid if you win? These are only examples in a vast sea of opportunity.

So let's be clear. Everything is done with a contract. There should not be a single person or company that you do business with if you do not have a contract. If they will not sign a contract, be very wary of doing business with them. I believe my word is my bond, and I live my life that way. But not every person does. Even though my word is sacred to me, I never hesitate to sign a contract stating what I will and will not do. Why? Because I understand the importance of this. If someone acts offended that you want to memorialize a verbal agreement in writing, this should be a red flag. By the way, verbal agreements over a certain value and/or pertaining to real property are **unenforceable** in many states. This means without that written contract you may be up a creek without a paddle. Get it in writing.

I hear clients all the time complain that they cannot hire a lawyer for every little thing. This is very true when you are just starting out. Get a lawyer to give you some basic contracts for basic situations. If you have to prepare a contract yourself, take time with it. Think about anything and everything that could go wrong. When you think it is perfect, put it away, go do something else, and then come back to it. You will be amazed at how many things you will think of during this off time. Even as attorneys, we rarely draft a contract in one sitting. Sure, the meat of it may be done at once, but I owe it to my client to sleep on it and make it the best agreement possible.

Choosing an Attorney—Just Like Choosing a Mate

The age of technology has changed the process of finding a lawyer. In the old days, you used to ask around until you found someone who knew a good lawyer. Maybe one lawyer in town has a sterling reputation. Now we all line up on the Internet to tell you how great we are. You can't really blame us. We live in a competitive business environment. So how do you separate the wheat from the chaff? I have a few suggestions for you:

- *Meet your lawyer.* If you can do this in person, please do. If you cannot, at least speak with them over the phone. Get a feel for their personality. Will your personality be compatible? You want someone you will get along with but who will give you the hard answers. A yes-man is not ideal in a lawyer, but you want to like speaking to them.
- *Get a clear understanding of what you are paying for and how much you are paying.* This sounds obvious, but it is harder to put into practice. Make sure you know what fee arrangement you have and what triggers billing. Is your lawyer going to bill you for every e-mail that comes in? Is your lawyer going to do something for a flat fee? If so, what do you get for that flat fee? Are they going to just give you a document and refuse to make revisions after that? If they are doing it hourly, will they agree to some sort of cap? Negotiating the bill on the front end is key. Most lawyers do not like it when a client calls them after a bill goes out—it feels as though it is an insult to the work they did. On the contrary, you will find that most lawyers are happy to have a discussion on the front end about fee expectations.
- *Referrals are golden if used correctly.* If a lawyer was referred to you, collect as much information as possible. Why is the lawyer being referred? What about that lawyer makes them desirable?
- *Referrals from other lawyers can be great.* Just ask the right questions. Sometimes people call me and need help with a legal problem that I just don't handle. I make it my business to know people whom I consider to be in the top of that field in my

region. Why? Because when I make a referral, my reputation is on the line. What if I refer a lawyer to you and he does a terrible job? It may not be my legal problem, but now you will always remember that my judgment is terrible. That is not what I want. So ask why they are referring that person. Is it just someone they know who does that type of work? Do they have any experience with that attorney in that context? Years ago I worked on a large matter with a number of attorneys. One in particular was a wealth management attorney. To be honest, I didn't even know what a wealth management attorney did until I met him. I was so impressed with what he did for our mutual client that I always recommend him to high-net-worth clients. That is the type of referral you want. You want someone to say, I was very impressed with their skill in that area and you should give them a call.

- *Go with your gut.* Have you ever been on a date with someone and just gotten a bit of an off feeling? Don't ignore that just because you think someone is a good lawyer. I can't tell you how many clients come to us after leaving another law firm and tell us that they had a bad feeling when they hired the other firm. That doesn't make the other lawyer a bad person. It just means that you knew in your heart of hearts that it was a bad fit. If you know that, why would you go there?

PROPERTY MANAGEMENT—FOCUSED BUSINESS PLAN

At this point, one of the most important things you can do is put your vision down on paper. It has been said that many people are born with sight, but what they lack is vision. Putting your vision down on paper in detail is what we are going to do here. I have provided for you in this section a complete property management–focused business plan.

CONTENTS

1.0 MISSION STATEMENT

When people ask you what you do, what do you tell them?

This mission statement should clearly define your purpose and should include the benefits your business provides. Do your research and come up with a solid mission statement. This is the "why" in your road trip.

Mission Statement

1.1 REAL ESTATE GOALS

Where do you want to go? What do you want real estate to help you to achieve?

If your goal is to make five thousand dollars per month in passive income, write that down. If your goal is to flip four homes per month, write that down. These goals may change over time, affecting the rest of your business plan, and that's okay. Make sure to put down both short- and long-term goals. By setting smaller, more achievable goals, you'll give yourself something to always look forward to accomplishing, and this will help you stay motivated.

Real Estate Goals

1.2 REAL ESTATE INVESTMENT STRATEGY

There are hundreds of ways to make money in real estate—but you don't need hundreds. You simply need to pick one strategy and become a master of it.

That strategy (vehicle), if dependable, will carry you through to your destination (your goals). If you are choosing to flip homes to generate cash in order to save up enough to quit your job, write that down. If you are looking to build passive income from small, multifamily properties for your retirement, write that down. Don't worry if you don't understand or know how you're going to accomplish everything in the plan. Remember, your business plan can and will change in time, and as you learn, you'll fill the plan out with more details.

Real Estate Investment Strategy

2.0 CRITERIA

Before you go out and start looking for deals, you need to establish the criteria those deals must meet.

You'll want to define your loan to value, cash flow requirements, max purchase amount, max rehab amount, max time frame, and so on (these are all items you'll pick up as we go further). One of the most important lessons you can possibly learn is to stick to your criteria and walk away from any deal that does not meet your criteria. It is very easy to become emotionally attached to a deal, but by sticking to your criteria, you take the emotion out of the picture.

Criteria

2.1 TIME FRAME

What is your time frame to reach your goal? Be realistic, but don't be afraid to reach, either. Do you want to retire in ten years? Are you planning on quitting your job next month?

Document your time line here. You can do this in accordance with your goals, as mentioned above.

Time Frame

2.2 RENTAL INVESTMENT MARKET

Define your market. What kind of property will you be looking for? Low income? High income? Commercial areas?

As a beginner, choose an area you feel most comfortable with. Most new investors should plan on investing within a short driving distance of home, rather than investing long-distance (unless your location makes it impossible to do otherwise). Doing this will help you to become an expert in that area, which will help you more easily analyze deals and opportunities. It will also help you know the players in the area, which will ultimately help you find partners—and, again, opportunities.

Rental Investment Market

2.3 PERSONAL FINANCES

Detail your personal finances.

Personal Finances	Amount

2.4 FINANCIAL ANALYSIS

How do you plan on acquiring your deals? Are you using conventional loans, hard money, private money, equity partners, seller financing, lease options, or some other creative method?

Finding financing is often a challenge in today's market, and private money provides a tremendous solution. Learn to attract private money so you've always got a steady cash flow when deals present themselves.

Financial Source	Amount

3.0 PROPERTY MANAGEMENT

(See operations manual)

- Marketing
- How to handle the day-to-day
- Moving your tenant in
- Maintenance
- Approaching the end of the lease term
- Organizing your files

3.1 TEAMS AND SYSTEMS

Clearly define your team and the systems you and they will use to delegate and automate tasks. Who will be on your team? Will you need an attorney, a CPA?

You don't necessarily need to know who those people are, simply what roles you will need filled on your team. More on this below.

Teams and Systems

EXIT STRATEGIES AND BACKUP PLANS

Having multiple clearly defined exit strategies is one of the most important parts of your business plan, especially for new investors. How are you going to exit the deal? What are your backup plans? Do you flip, lease option, wholesale, bird-dog, sell the note, sell the entity holding title, rent and hold, or some other technique? What is the end game?

This needs to be clearly defined.

Exit Strategies and Backup Plans

EXAMPLE DEALS

One of the parts of the business plan that seems to get new investors excited is the illustration of the future of the business.
What would an ideal but feasible next ten years look like?

Illustrate purchases, cash flow, appreciation, sales, trades, 1031 exchanges, cash-on-cash return, and more to demonstrate what your path might look like. This goes somewhat hand in hand with your goals—it just illustrates possible ways of making them happen.

Additionally, this will change with time because, of course, ideals are not real life. However, it is good to see what is possible.

Example Deals	

FINANCIALS

Include a personal description of where your financials are today. What do you bring to the table? Do you have any equity you can use? Are you starting with nothing?

Document your current situation and update it as often as it changes. As you move forward with your investments, it is always important to have at the ready your complete financials.

Financials	

ONE LAST THING

Remember that road maps and business plans are guides, not rules. A business plan is meant to give you direction and to motivate you to follow it. When you have a clearly defined business plan, carrying out the plan and envisioning the end becomes much more attainable.

It is almost impossible to follow a financial or real estate road map perfectly. While you can plot your course with care and extreme precision, there are still many outside forces at play. However, your road map is designed to keep you headed in the right direction at the correct speed. You may come across bumps in the road, dead ends, and even a breakdown or two. However, if you hold as tightly as you can to the map you've created, you will pass through those problems and come out at your destination.

If you talk to investors who have failed in this business, you'll find that the majority of them did so primarily because of a lack of preparation and planning. Don't fall into this trap.

ASSEMBLING YOUR TEAM

While as an investor you are required to wear many different hats, you don't need to (and can't) wear all of them. Instead, you need a team. When we refer to "team," we're not suggesting you go out and hire a team of employees to work under you. A "team" is merely a collection of individuals in various different businesses whom you can rely on to help you move your business forward. Here's a brief look at who should be on any winning real estate investing team:

Your mentor: Every successful entrepreneur needs a good mentor, a guide. By training under the watchful eye of one smarter than us, we can only get smarter.

Mortgage broker/loan officer: A mortgage broker is the person responsible for getting you loans—especially if you are going "conventional" (not hard or private money). You want someone who has the experience of working with other investors, and you want that person to be creative and smart. Many loan officers have a pipeline of buyers (or future buyers); real estate investors can use the help of local loan officers to build a list of buyers and lease purchasers for their properties.

Real estate attorney: It is important to have someone on the team who can go through contracts and who knows the legalities of all your moves. Don't try to pinch pennies by ignoring this valuable member of your team. You don't need to meet for hours with your attorney each week, but you want someone to be available when you need them. Having an attorney who is skilled with real estate investing is highly important for the success of your career. Keep in mind that attorneys can also be compensated through fees collected at acquisition or disposition of a property.

Escrow officer or title rep: If you live in a state that uses title and escrow companies, your escrow officer or title rep is the person responsible for closing the deal, taking you from "the offer" to "the keys." Having a good one on the team helps to close deals that much quicker. You always want people looking out for *your* interests.

Accountant: As you acquire properties, doing your own taxes and bookkeeping becomes increasingly difficult. As soon as possible, hire an accountant (preferably a certified public accountant). Your numbers person should also be well aware of the ins and outs of real estate and preferably own rental properties of their own. Come tax time, this is the person to help you through the write-offs. A good tax accountant will save you more than they cost.

Insurance agent: Insurance is a must, and as an investor, you will probably be dealing with a lot of insurance policies. Be sure to shop around for both the best rates and the best service. Do not skimp on getting insurance, as you never know when you'll need that policy.

Contractor: A good contractor seems like the hardest team member to find, but can often make or break your profit margin. You want someone who gets things done on time and under budget! Be sure that your contractor is licensed/bonded/insured to protect you. Don't simply hire the cheap guy.

Supportive family and friends: Having the support and backing of loved ones is important in any endeavor. If your spouse or family is not on board, don't invest until they are.

Realtor: An exceptional real estate agent is fundamental in your investing career. You or your spouse may even choose to become a real estate agent yourself to gain access to the incredible tools that agents have. Either way, having an agent who is punctual, a go-getter, and eager is important. Real estate agents are paid from the commission when a property is sold. In other words: for the buyer, an agent is *free*. They can be an excellent resource for contract real estate work, which may include the following activities: bird dogging, referring buyers, showing properties, open houses, broker price opinions, and so on.

Property manager: If you don't want to actively manage your properties, a good property manager is important to have. A good property manager can be hard to find, but finding one who can efficiently manage your rentals will make your life significantly easier.

Great handyperson: Someone to take care of the little things that come up on a daily basis is imperative. Ask for referrals from other landlords for the best around; they typically don't need to advertise, but work almost entirely on referrals from a small group of investors and homeowners.

One of the best sources for finding these team members is through referrals from other investors. In general, another investor would be happy to refer their handyperson, mortgage broker, or accountant to you because it reflects well on themselves and their relationship with that professional. Try asking around at your local real estate investor club or on Landlord Academy, and you'll be well on your way toward putting the pieces in place.

WHAT MAKES A GREAT REAL ESTATE TEAM?

A great real estate team is defined by its ability to consistently produce reliable *results*. As you might suspect, that's way more difficult to make a reality than it is to talk about.

Investors, especially ones with either large portfolios or those who flip a lot (often both), rely on their team daily. When one member fails, the entire endeavor suffers, sometimes to the point of sabotaging the team's goals altogether. Whether you're serving clients, flipping properties, or keeping track of your rentals, your team must consistently produce and avoid the "excuse train" at all costs. There are those who do—and those who make excuses. The latter will pull you down faster than you can imagine.

People talk a good game, so watch them when it's their turn to produce. A great team member should exhibit certain traits, which are sometimes difficult to see on the surface but can be witnessed through longer conversations and via referrals from others. For example:

- Are they really experts?
- Do they interact well with everyone?
- Are they a pain to contact?
- Do they return calls/e-mails quickly?
- Do they hit deadlines?
- Do they produce as promised, when promised?
- Can they communicate clearly and efficiently?

Assembling the team will not happen overnight, but once together, they will give you the backing and help you'll need to make your real estate investing dreams come true.

THE EXTRA STEP AFTER COMPLETING YOUR BUSINESS PLAN: UNDERSTAND HOW YOUR BUSINESS WILL MAKE MONEY

As a property management business, you may want to create a point system to help grade a rental project and its presumed value. This will help dictate the fee structure for your management agreement. What seems like a good project may not be worth the time investment or the investment in operating cost to the business.

Things to consider:

- *Client relationship:* How many properties do they own? Are there other opportunities that working with them can provide?
- *Property asset class:* Are these single family or apartment buildings?
- *Property location:* Is this in a high-crime location that will require more of your resources to manage and maintain?
- *Owner interview results:* Does this seem like an active owner? How much of your time will they consume? Are they the pain-in-the-ass owner who is going to micromanage and urgently call you at all hours for minor issues?

A well-built property management company will generate monthly income from the following sources:

- *Application fees:* Through the Landlord Academy's partnership with TransUnion's SmartMove, you can charge prospects an additional fee over and above the hard cost to complete the tenant screening process. For example, if the average screen of a prospect tenant costs $35, you can charge the prospect $60, making a net profit of $25. Multiply this by several screens a week and you can generate a considerable amount of income.
- *Leasing fees:* Typically, a management company will charge a portion of the first month's rent as a lease-up. I recommend charging 100 percent of the first month's rent, unless you have a great relationship with the property owner and want to reduce the fee to 50 percent of the monthly rent. For simple math, this fee split will look like this: If monthly rent equals $1,000, a 50 percent lease-up fee will equal a $500 net profit to the property management company.
- *Renewal fees:* Renewal fees are applied at the end of every lease term. I recommend charging the property owner between 30 percent and 50 percent of the monthly rent per renewed lease. Going back to the previous example, if a rental unit was leased for $1,000, the property management company would receive $500 at the end of the

lease term once the tenant renews the lease. Keep in mind that with each renewal the rent should increase based on market conditions. This ultimately increases the net operating income, which will affect the management fee positively, as management fees are typically attached to the gross operating income of the rental.

- *Late payment fees:* When a tenant pays rent late, a late fee is assessed, which ranges between $50 and $100 or more, of which the management company receives a negotiated percentage.

- *Maintenance fees:* Because a good property management company handles the majority of the maintenance issues on the property, I recommend that the management company receive a percentage of the fee charged to the property owner by the contractor who actually completes the maintenance work. When I have employed this practice in my property management company, I made sure that the owner was made aware of my fee. Also keep in mind that the owner did not pay a higher price for the services, as the maintenance technician/contractor had simply reduced their fee in order to remain competitive in the market. This agreement was also beneficial for the contractors because of the sheer amount of business we referred to them on a monthly basis. Some property management companies choose to hire a full-time contractor/maintenance technician, but you may choose to subcontract to reduce costs.

- *Management fees:* This is typically attached to the gross operating income of the rental unit. So if the rental property is listed for $1,000 a month and the management company charges 10 percent, the management company would receive $100 a month as a management fee. This is where property management companies tend to make most—if not all—of their revenue, but hopefully you can now see that there are many other ways to generate income for your company. And keep in mind all of the above items are negotiable. As I have often said, you don't get paid what you are worth, you only get paid what you negotiate.

- *Transaction commissions:* There will be opportunity for your services to provide income from transactions. It is a good idea to be able to capture these as they can increase income as well as provide additional properties under management.

In addition to leveraging multiple income streams from the same property, you may also want to consider diversifying your management portfolio and taking on vacation rentals, commercial buildings, warehouses, and other rental properties. You should also remember that, as a property manager, the amount of referrals from tenants and owners that you will receive is tremendous. In my opinion, property management is one of the greatest sources of lead generation there is for any real estate brokerage.

Building a successful property management company is simple, but it's not easy. As with launching any business, there will be ups and downs, trials and triumphs, and in my experience, I have learned that your best defense against the roller coaster of entrepreneurship is your mind. The qualities you need to be successful in property management are the same qualities you need to be successful in any other area of life—discipline, focus, execution, commitment to fundamentals, and perseverance. Those are the staples, and it starts with you.

PART II

YOUR PROPERTY MANAGEMENT BUSINESS PLAN

WHAT'S YOUR WHY?

Determining your vision and writing an executive summary

Nobody likes writing business plans anymore. They think it's a waste of time and just another task that's keeping them from making money. I disagree. I know that having a solid plan is crucial to business success, and my absolute favorite part of the business plan is the executive summary.

A lot of people like to skip right past this brief section of the business plan to get right to the detailed marketing and operations plans. And while I agree that those sections are important (we'll cover those next), I truly believe that a well-written business plan is the lifeblood of a growing business. At the same time, a company that has a poorly written executive summary—or none at all—is likely headed for trouble. So what's *really* so important about the executive summary? Let's take a look.

An executive summary should detail a company's objectives, mission statement, and keys to success, and it sets the groundwork to help everyone close to the organization understand the company's main purpose. Essentially, a good executive summary answers the questions *Who are you?* and *Why are you here?*

WHO ARE YOU AND WHY ARE YOU HERE?

When I started out in property management, I would take on properties in impoverished neighborhoods just because I wanted to prove to people that I could stabilize those properties and start turning a massive profit. My heart wasn't in it, though, and I would start to feel resentful that I was doing work that I didn't really enjoy. And I hear the same stories from other property managers all the time. Their passion is in vacation rentals, but all of a sudden they find themselves with a portfolio of Section 8 properties because it seemed like easy money. Or they wanted to focus on revitalizing low-income neighborhoods, but they're managing a bunch of luxury condos instead. There's nothing wrong with managing Section 8 properties or luxury condos—as long as they fit in with your initial vision for your company. If not, and you're taking on properties just to make a quick buck or to show off your management skills, your blessing will quickly become a curse.

When you start a business, you're hungry. You're trying to find something that sticks so you can start a profit. And that's okay. Everyone starts there. But I see a lot of real estate entrepreneurs become slaves to their bills instead of focusing on the company's goal and purpose. When you don't have an executive summary that lays out the company's focus, plans, and objectives, you quickly start bouncing back and forth like a pinball, jumping to whatever opportunity will provide the biggest check. In the early days of your business, there will be many tasks and opportunities that will beg to become your new focus point, but the point of the executive summary is to say, "This is why we started this company, and this what we're here to do."

WHEN YOU BUILD IT, THEY WILL COME

The other primary focus of the executive summary is to help everyone else working with your company to stay aware of the company's mission and objectives. This is not a huge issue when you're working alone, or with one other partner who builds the company from scratch with you. But as you begin to add other property managers and professionals to your team, it is absolutely critical that they understand the DNA of your company. At Nike, even the janitor knows the mission statement of the company because it's embedded in the culture. And think about your favorite athletic team—the team's mission statement or tagline is painted right over the door for all the players to see as they enter the locker room or arena. You see team members tapping or rubbing this mantra as they walk past it, and while it doesn't seem that important, it actually represents the very identity of the entire organization. And when the team is down by fifteen with five minutes left in the fourth quarter, the coach reminds the players of that mission statement, and that's what keeps everybody going. Every single player on the field immediately digs deep and finds their second wind because they've all bought into the team's vision. A solid executive summary should do this for your company as well.

One of my coaching clients recently started a property management company, and she started growing really quickly—so quickly, in fact, that she had to bring in someone else to help with management. Unfortunately, things went downhill in a hurry. My client was frustrated because she started her business to service luxury clients, and she had this vision for white-glove service and a high-end company culture, but she couldn't understand why her new hire wasn't executing this vision. My client complained that her new manager didn't understand her company's mission, and she was right. But she didn't understand that it wasn't the manager's fault—it was her fault.

When I asked my client to go back and show me her executive summary, in which she clearly detailed the overall mission and vision for her company, she couldn't produce it. She had never written it, she said, because she didn't think it was that important. Suddenly, though, as she sat on the brink of losing many of her clients almost as quickly as she had gotten them, she realized how important it was.

WHAT'S YOUR VISION?

Before we go into detail about operations systems and screening tenant prospects, I want you to take some time to get crystal clear about your vision for your new property management company. You may not have all of the answers now, but start by taking some notes. Think about your background and strengths and the experience that you bring to the market that can give you a competitive edge among other property managers. Think about your ideal client and why and how you want to serve them. Think about what the perfect day looks like for you as you run your company—are you out in the field, visiting properties? Are you in the office taking client calls and trying to secure new business? Or have you grown your company to the point that you're not very hands-on at all, and you actually spend most of your time delegating to other individuals while you vacation with your family or volunteer with local charities? All these are important questions to ask because they will help you craft the executive summary that will keep your company on track through good times and bad, help you to avoid distractions, and ensure that every new team member is as plugged-in to the company's core beliefs as you are.

I don't think there's an ideal template for an executive summary. Yours might be three pages long while someone else's is only three paragraphs. What matters is that you actually record all the necessary details so that it can be posted in a highly visible location and be reproduced to disseminate as needed. Remember that executive summaries are only effective when they are seen and implemented.

I do believe, however, that we can learn a lot from others who have gone before, so I do want to share the stories of some successful property managers who discovered their unique selling proposition and leveraged it to create tremendous growth for their companies. These are not their actual executive summaries, but these statements do clearly demonstrate their company's vision and purpose. Their philosophies and management styles may differ from your own, but you can get a feel for what resonates with you and what doesn't. Read through these and let them be your guide as you draft your own executive summary.

DANIEL J. HYMAN—CHAIRMAN & CEO, MILLENNIUM PROPERTIES R/E

Nearly twenty years ago, I started Millennium Properties R/E as an independent brokerage and property management firm that would target smaller owners and institutional clients. We work with all types of commercial properties in Chicago and throughout the Midwest, including neighborhood retail centers, apartment complexes, office buildings, industrial warehouses, and commercial condos.

I had twenty years of brokerage experience prior to starting the firm, much of it working with noninstitutional owners. These types of owners—many of whom control only a few properties—are typically ignored by the big-name brokerage firms due to their potential deal size and volume of transactions. As I built the company, I decided that it is better for us to sell $5 million through a number of deals than wait and hope that we could get a single $5 million listing. I am personally known as an aggressive person, and we have built a culture at this firm that reflects that drive and determination. Early on, we even chose purple for our logo and branding to help distinguish our signs and marketing materials from all of the other firms that tend to use red and blue as their primary brand colors.

Millennium really saw huge growth after the market collapse in 2008. Before that point, we had always had a niche business representing banks and the courts on receivership properties. After the downturn, our business surged with an explosion of sale listings and properties under management; as a result, our company tripled in size within four years. We were not very well prepared for the surge of business, and it took us some time to find the right employees to meet the demanding workload. It's really a tough mix to get the right people in the right roles. The one thing I think we could have done better was to hire a controller and a head of property management earlier than I did. Since I did not want to be overstaffed, I played it a bit too cautiously in terms of staffing, as I do not like to let people go.

Several of our brokers had previous experience as property managers, so as the downturn happened, they were well prepared to move into receivership management. The management team was also comprised of driven people who were eager to accept the challenge of managing a large portfolio with a wide array of property types. Our aggressive culture encourages people to meet the market as it stands. As many individuals stopped selling postrecession, we targeted the banks for an increased number of sale listings. This strategy has continued to benefit us, as not only do we have a large number of financial institution clients, we also have a number of value-add investors who are interested in buying our listings.

As the markets have continued to recover, we are again shifting our strategy, as we are approaching value-add investors to see whether they are ready to capture the gains from the improved property market from when we originally sold the property to them. We have also shifted the focus of our management business in the last eighteen months. This shift has seen us trim staff and pursue more third-party management assignments, which is something we could not do when we were solely focused on REO management.

New property managers need to consider whether they want to exclusively focus on operating properties or whether they want to be involved in leasing their assignments as well. By doing just management operations, you can get business referrals from other brokers in the market. As a firm that does both leasing and operations, we have to target owners and pitch our management services directly to them. Managers also need to consider whether they want to specialize in only one type of property—multifamily, retail, office, or industrial. There are also firms that exclusively manage condo associations. Many firms specialize by targeting just one of these markets; however, we manage many of these in addition to the mixed-use buildings that frequently include apartments and retail or office space.

Bank-owned properties were and are the core of our management business. Our management business was very small prior to 2008. We were a predominantly brokerage business prior to the downturn. As a result, most of our management experience has been bank-owned and receivership properties. That year saw the launch of our management business when it shifted from a way to cover overhead to a substantial profit center. Our management business also allowed us to be the first choice as the broker when the bank decided to sell properties that we had under management. The upside of bank-owned properties is that when a market downturn happens, there is an increase in business, making it recession-proof. The downside is that the management assignments can be on a very short cycle with sometimes as little as nine to eighteen months before you lose an assignment.

MARK AINLEY—OWNER AND FOUNDER, GC REALTY AND DEVELOPMENT AND GC REALTY INVESTMENTS

I have been an active property manager since 2005, and my company currently manages around seven hundred residential units and about one million square feet of commercial space. Much of our growth has been centered on working with owners with troubled properties and the redevelopment of distressed properties for our own portfolio. We have made a habit of turning these properties around and restoring them to cash-flowing assets for our clients and ourselves.

Since 2005 we have experienced a couple of cycles of growth—the first being when we transitioned into property management from being solely a brokerage company. We did it with the intention of smoothing out our cash flows with monthly recurring revenue. The cash flow starts to become real with property management when you start getting above a couple of hundred doors. At this point, you begin to have systems in place to handle the day-to-day operations, and unlike a brokerage, a property management business has checks coming in every week. They are smaller checks, but they are more consistent, so every month you have a good idea of how much cash will be on hand. With a brokerage you are always chasing your next check.

For us, the most difficult aspect of transitioning to a property management business was in creating consistency through processes and managing people. The funny thing about being a property manager is that it has little to do with managing properties but everything to do with managing people. And, sometimes, the people are difficult. When I had brokers working for me, I didn't need to manage them. If they didn't sell anything, they didn't get paid—everyone was out there hustling on their own. With property management, however, I have to keep everyone on task. Still, I don't think the process of transitioning was all that difficult, because I had a good background in multiple areas of the real estate industry.

Our next cycle of growth began around 2010, when we started redeveloping properties for our own portfolio. My and my partner's time began to stretch thin and we were unable to keep up with everything. A new partner joined our group a little after that and really introduced the idea of delegation, process mapping, and systemization, thus allowing our business to grow to the next level.

My newest partner actually sought us out. We started investing side by side with him, and the business kept growing. We all went with the intention of buying a few properties and then reevaluating, but it kept going, and as our investment business continued to grow, he started becoming more involved in the property management aspect of the business because he was our biggest client. He was interested in improving his own returns, which, in turn, helped us out, along with all of our clients. What made things really easy is that we all complemented one another. After being in bad partnerships, my first partner and I finally realized what a good partnership was with him. When we met him, our business was kind of at a transition point. We were in need of structure, so when he came on, there was almost a creation of a new culture. We began to see things from a different perspective. We had been working together for a few years, and he contributed so much to our business, we felt like not making him a partner would cost us more money than what we gave up.

KEVIN ORTNER—CEO, RENTERS WAREHOUSE

I joined Renters Warehouse in 2009 when I opened the very first Renters Warehouse franchise in Phoenix, Arizona. My franchise was consistently awarded with best-in-class business and culture awards, and reached two thousand properties under management in 2016—a record for a single franchise.

In 2015, after the retirement of Renters Warehouse founder Brenton Hayden, I took on the reins of the entire company and have led it to immense growth since then. We are currently one of the largest and most awarded property management firms in the United States, managing more than 17,000 homes for more than 13,500 investors across the country—a total of about $3 billion worth of residential real estate.

When I started out in property management, I didn't want to reinvent the wheel. I saw that Renters Warehouse was doing things differently and was excited to help shape that. I got in early enough that I had influence on how the business was built, but also, I didn't have to start from scratch. Sure, we could have opened up our own company and started our own brand, but being a part of something bigger was exciting, and some of the early legwork was done. That's the benefit of opening a franchise business rather than starting from square one. It was the right decision for us, but again, we chose a company that had already aligned with our vision and we were in a position to be able to help shape and influence the product offering and growth over time.

But even without a brand like Renters Warehouse, you can still establish a successful company. The key is hard work and persistence. As with any business, clients don't come easy. This is a highly fragmented and competitive industry, so our clients have lots of options. Remember, it is far more difficult and expensive to find new clients than it is to keep your current clients. So, ensure you are working hard to deliver on-brand promises to those you have already sold. Your brand is everything. There are more than two hundred thousand third-party property managers across the United States, so competition is fierce. If you tarnish your brand with poor service, it's next to impossible to come back from that. Protect your brand, even if it means growing the business a little slower than you would like.

Early on in the development of the Phoenix Renters Warehouse franchise, like most early-stage businesses, we grew our client base by pounding the pavement—getting out and selling. We were attending networking events, cold-calling potential clients, and building a better value proposition. We ran an honest business and delivered on the promises we made to our clients. This later allowed us to attract great talent to the company, as people want to work for great brands and great businesses. Once we started building a team of amazing people, the business and culture awards followed. At the end of the day, strong business success and growth come down to having the right people in your business driving toward a common vision.

STEVE SHWETZ, MANAGING BROKER, MESA PROPERTY MANAGEMENT INC.

In 2009, in the midst of the housing crisis, I had a goal of buying two rental properties in the Southern California market known as the High Desert, which includes the cities of Hesperia, Victorville, and Apple Valley. I chose this area because the values in this market had dropped well over 50 to 60 percent, compared to about 20 to 25 percent in the area I lived in. The market was also only fifty miles from my home, and I could still be personally involved in buying, rehabbing, and, if necessary, managing any properties I eventually turned into buy-and-hold rentals.

During this time, I was rehabbing properties, and I was also researching property management companies to manage my buy-and-holds. The companies servicing my area were not very owner-friendly. I thought they charged too much money, were too slow to distribute owner funds, and did not do a very good job of screening tenants. All but three of the property management companies were primarily real estate sales offices and did not focus primarily on property management.

Most real estate agents hate managing rental units. It's not very sexy; the commission is nothing compared to a sale (in the short term); and working with a tenant is *very* different from working with buyers and sellers. Having a traditional real estate sales office manage your income property is like asking a concierge at a hotel to work as a prison guard. They have a high probability of getting killed.

After looking at their websites and doing a Google search for property management companies in my area, I saw a huge opportunity. Most companies were living like it was 1999 in terms of their online presence. Nobody was doing anything to actively market for owners on the web, yet the search volume on Google showed owners were actively looking for property management companies. It was a perfect opportunity to start a company.

My biggest early client was myself. I eventually bought and kept twenty-seven units. Along the way my hard-money lender decided part of his strategy to recover from the recession would be to buy and hold rentals. He also had about fifteen homes he had taken back from a builder when the market collapsed, and we took over the management of those properties. During the flip phase of the business I worked with other investors who wanted to own rather than flip, so I offered to manage both the rehab and the long-term management of the properties. Most of those clients are still with us today.

Another set of early owners were those homeowners who needed/wanted to move but didn't want to sell their homes at the current depressed prices. For them, renting their properties was a way to wait out the market for a recovery. Many of those owners are selling their homes when the tenant moves out.

All told, we went from start-up to managing more than six-hundred single-family homes, condos, and apartments in Southern California in little more than five years.

I'm not sure we will ever see as good a time to start a property management business as we did in 2009, but any time is a great time to start a business if there is demand for your product or service and the competition is weak. Not every market is as good as the high desert of Southern California, with a relatively high percentage of nonowner-occupied units and marginal vendors servicing the market—but you can still start and grow in a smaller market with stronger competitors. In 2016 we opened our second office in a market just like that, and we have been able to grow in that market, too. It's a slower process, but it can be done.

Anybody looking to get into property management today needs to position their business to be focused on their customer's needs. Your customer is *not* the tenant: it's the owner. Our philosophy is that we only make money on our management fees and we only collect our fee if the tenant is paying rent. We don't mark up invoices. What the owner would pay the vendor, we charge that and nothing more. We are also very strict on rent collection. Rent is due on the first and late on the second. Unless the tenant has called us in advance about a promise to pay, they are immediately getting a three-day pay rent or quit notice.

Regarding the need for property managers, I think it is here to stay for the long term. Home ownership is at the lowest level since the early 1960s, and "the experts" say that's not going to change anytime soon. Somebody has to manage all those tenants, so it might as well be you!

MASTERING THE DAY-TO-DAY

Identifying the work that needs to be done and creating operating procedures

At this point, you have a clear understanding of what it takes to become a successful entrepreneur, as well as a good idea about how you're going to structure your new property management business. Now it's time to learn what it will take to run your business on a day-to-day basis.

The following day-to-day procedures represent the more common components of an operations manual. This template has been developed over the course of fifteen years of my consulting and personal experience in setting up property management businesses. Simply put, this template operations manual will identify the work that needs to be done by the property manager and then tell the property manager how to go about performing that work in a consistent manner. When you can consistently perform the required steps, your company will be compliant and profitable. As I have often said, we can all make a better hamburger than McDonald's, but none of us will sell 5 million hamburgers in a day. One of the reasons they are able to do this is that they have proper systems in place. The secret to success is not necessarily based on experience, it is more so based on your operation systems.

The company's vision, mission statement, values, and purpose may be included in the introduction to the manual. The following bullet points are things you may want to consider and include in your manual:

- Company policies
- Office policies and procedures
- Computer and information technology policies (including ownership of information)
- Leasing procedures
- Maintenance procedures
- Construction supervision or coordination policies and procedures

Before we begin, I have an **important disclaimer**:

Please be advised that industry regulations vary from state to state. Accordingly, it is imperative that you thoroughly review any and all such laws and regulations in your state, as well as their impact on your ongoing business activities. This manual is designed solely for informational purposes and is not intended and shall not be deemed to offer or provide legal (or other) advice or guidance. You should obtain your own legal advice from qualified legal professionals. The Landlord Property Management Academy makes no representations or warranties that the procedures covered in this manual comply with any laws, rules, or regulations that may exist in or be applicable to your jurisdiction.

Now we're ready.

FIRST CONTACT, QUALIFYING, AND APPROVING A PROSPECT TENANT

SECTION 1

Before you are ready to lease your rental property, you need to decide on the following things. Check with your local fair housing agency for any jurisdiction-specific requirements.

- What monthly rent are you going to charge?
- What is your application fee?
- What is your security deposit amount?
- Are you requiring first and/or last month's rent?
- What credit score are you requiring?
- What type of criminal record will you accept, if any?
- Are you allowing pets? If so, what kind and what are you charging?

💡 BRYAN'S TIP: What to Charge for Rent 💡

Rent must cover at least these items:

- Mortgage payments
- Taxes
- Insurance
- Interest payments
- Estimated vacancy loss (at least 5 percent if you have more than one rental property)
- Utilities provided by landlord (if any)
- Collection expenses
- Legal and accounting fees
- Advertising

TIPS: Maximizing Your Rental Amount

Determining how much you can charge for rent is a tricky game. If you charge too much, your unit will sit empty. If you undercharge, you are losing money that you may need one day for repairs or other expenses. The Landlord Property Management Academy offers resources and tools to help you determine market surveys. For more information on this process please visit our website, www.landlordacademy.com. Go to the Tools section for tips on how to locate rental rates. Most of the information required here should have already been gathered in your SEOTA process. When it comes to rents, you will want to perform a streamlined version of the SEOTA, most commonly known as a market survey. You should perform a market survey no less than once a week to make sure you are setting your rents at a rate that will be attractive to your prospective tenant. Remember: setting rents is a science—you must know your market as well as your rental unit(s) to make sure you're not only competitive but also realistic with what you are asking for as a rental rate.

When running a property, you need to take different things into consideration at different times:

- When to rent a unit for the first time
- When to determine how much to raise the rent, prior to the end of a lease term
- When to decide whether to rent or sell a property
- When to rent through the Section 8 program

Remember: you can only raise the rent at the end of a lease term, so if you don't get it right, you may have to wait the entire lease term to change it!

💡   BRYAN'S TIP: Single-Family Homes   💡

I recommend that landlords renting out single-family dwellings ask for a security deposit equal to one month's rent, plus first and last month's rent in advance.

Single-family means just that: one household. There is more risk and little mistakes can be costlier. You don't have the luxury of other rental units bringing income, as in a multi-family complex that will offset your vacancy loss for one empty unit. So cover every angle by collecting a month's rent in advance. You don't need any surprises, but if one should arise, you will be more prepared with 30 to 45 percent of the total rate.

With vacation rentals, you will want to receive a deposit up front. Best practice is to take a percentage of the full daily, weekly rate. A typical rate is 30 to 40 percent of the total rate.

SECTION 2: FIRST CONTACT WITH PROSPECTIVE TENANT

💻 TIPS: Technology Hacks— 💻
Marketing Your Rental Unit and Its First Impression

Be prepared for your first interaction with your prospective tenant (prospect). It is important that before you receive a phone call or e-mail from them, you have put thought into their first impression of your property's marketing. When you are putting your property online on various sites such as Zillow, there are a few strategies to use:

- Clean or stage the property
- Quality over quantity of pictures: Make sure they highlight the important amenities for the tenant. Include pictures of each bedroom, walk-in closets, front of the property, yard, bathrooms, garage, kitchens, and so forth. If you leave out important features or basic expectations, you will lose potential leads.
- Add a video of your unit. This will help people see the floor plan and whether it is a good fit for them. It will also be beneficial when you have a tenant moving. You can effectively market the unit before that tenant is out, saving you time and money.
- Provide all necessary information relevant to the tenant. Let your technology aid in the screening process. Do not waste your own time or theirs with misleading advertising.

💻 TIPS: Technology Hacks 💻

Be prepared for contact from prospective tenants. Having systems in place will help you stay in compliance with fair housing laws as well as improve efficiency and lead conversions.

Step 1: Have the pertinent information below available when a prospect calls:

1. Address of property
2. General area of town property is in and what is nearby (attractions, hospitals, shopping, etc.)
3. Type of dwelling (single-family house, town house, duplex)
4. Square footage
5. Number of bedrooms and bathrooms
6. Amenities (washer/dryer, pool, garage, etc.)
7. Pets allowed?
8. When is property available for move-in?

9. Rental rate
10. How much down? (security deposit, first month's rent, etc.)

Your rates will change weekly and sometimes daily depending on the season. So you will need to have your rates available to quote. Always be ready to offer promotional discounts and special offers to keep the prospect visiting your website often.

Step 2: When you receive your initial contact from a prospective tenant, you will use the phone card or your CRM software. Your goal will be to get as much information about the prospect as possible from this first phone call. You can use this information to help prequalify the prospect by explaining all rental prices, application fees, and deposits.

PHONE CARD

Date: _____

Name: _____

Address: _____

Telephone: (H) _____ (W) _____

Type of rental home desired: _____

How many will live in home: _____

Price range (optional): _____

Date needed: _____

Pets: _____

Why moving: _____

Comments: _____

How did you hear about us?

❏ Referral

❏ Newspaper   ❏ Flyer/Brochure

❏ For Rent sign   ❏ Locator service

❏ Yellow pages

Other: _____

Appointment scheduled: _____

Study Session: Phone Techniques

When your phone rings, be ready to focus on the task at hand. Make sure you are ready to answer the questions of the phone prospect. Your phone card should be used as a tool. Try not to read the phone card word for word. Look at it as a guide to help you touch on some of the important subjects.

Listen to the prospect. Understand their needs and adjust your conversation around their needs. If they are not clear, then ask questions designed to help discover what is most important to them. Get their full name. It's hard to connect with someone and discover their needs without first getting to know their name.

Sample questions:

1. "May I ask your name, please?"
2. "And your name is?"
3. "I apologize. What did you say your name was?"
4. "Sir or madam, your name is . . . ?"
5. "When are you looking to move?"
6. "What size home are you looking for?"
7. "Are you new to the area?"

Try to get only the information you need right then and there. You can get all the other details once the prospect commits to an appointment to see your rental unit.

Be clear that the prospect knows how to find your rental unit. Always be ready to provide clear directions. Also explain to the prospect how they will benefit from setting up an appointment with you to see the rental unit.

Sample explanations:

1. "We will be able to have a one-on-one conversation with no interruptions."
2. "You will be able to better plan your day knowing exactly how long it will take to see the rental unit. Making an appointment means I will be available and ready to show the unit so you won't have to wait!"

🖥 TIPS: Technology Hack 🖥

A professional phone reception service can be beneficial for your company no matter the size. At Chavis Realty, we use Ruby Receptionist for several reasons. Virtual receptionists eliminate the costly need for employing a flesh-and-blood receptionist at your company while allowing you to wear the many hats of a property manager:

· Calls are answered by a real person
· Calls are answered with a script designed by you that can provide pertinent information
· Contact information and messages are taken and e-mailed to you if you are not available
· The app tracks information

Step 1: If your first contact with your prospective tenant is in person, you will use the guest card or your CRM software. This should be used in conjunction with showing the apartment or home. Like the phone card, this form should be filled out as completely as possible. You can use many of the same questions above to relate to your prospect.

Step 2: If at the end of your conversation, your prospective tenant is interested in renting your property, schedule a time to meet the prospect to prequalify and show the property. If possible, make this time during the day so they can get a clear view of the property in daylight. Also give them the address and ask them to go by and look at the outside of the property and the neighborhood. Ask them to call you back after doing so if they are still interested.

Step 3: If the prospect does not call back in a few days, you call them! Some people are indecisive. Perhaps your call or demonstration of interest in them is all they need to bring them around to making a decision.

GUEST CARD

Date: _____

Name: _____

Address: _____

Telephone: (H) _____ (W) _____

Type of rental home desired: _____

How many will live in home: _____

Price range (optional): _____

Date needed: _____

Pets: _____

Why moving: _____

Comments: _____

How did you hear about us?

❏ Referral

❏ Newspaper   ❏ Flyer/Brochure

❏ For Rent sign   ❏ Locator service

❏ Yellow pages

Other: _____

Appointment scheduled: _____

After gathering the information on the prospect and filling out either a guest or phone card, you will need to enter the information into your property management software. This is a very important step to ensure that the information gathered can be tracked.

Property management software will help to:

- remind property manager to follow up
- track vital information on the prospect

- keep track of prospect traffic
- allow you to track marketing

SECTION 3: READYING YOUR UNIT AND YOURSELF FOR SHOWING

Most of today's property managers have lost the art of staging a rental unit; now most just take a few pictures and post to their rental listing platform of choice. As a professional property manager you will take a much more strategic approach to advertising your rentals. One key technique is to take well-thought-out pictures of the rental unit, showing all the bedrooms, bathrooms, closets, and storage areas. Do not forget to include any garage and/or yard space as well.

Step 1: Appeal to the senses of the prospect.

- Plug in fragrances
- Vacuum away footsteps so nice, clean vacuum lines show
- Have light refreshments (bottled water, cookies, etc.)
- Play soothing music such as jazz, classical, or nature sounds
- Have bright lighting

Step 2: Have good curb appeal. Most prospects make their decision within the first few moments of seeing your property. That is why the curb appeal, or what the property looks like when you first drive up to it, is so important.

- Clear away any trash from your yard or curb
- Make sure the grass is cut
- Make sure there is no junk or old items in the yard or otherwise visible
- Have a good paint job
- Make sure the window dressings (curtains, drapes, blinds, etc.) look nice from the outside view
- Have some landscaping

Step 3: Have a leasing folder with all the items you may need. These items can be added to your tablet, using available apps for easy access and for getting required signatures.

- Floor plans
- Community information
- Photographs
- Maps of the city for new tenant
- Applications

- Guest cards
- Qualifying criteria
- Move-in cost sheet
- Lease
- Pen
- Paper

SECTION 4: QUALIFYING PROSPECT AND SHOWING YOUR PROPERTY

Step 1: You will want to "qualify" your prospect before showing them the property. Use a qualifying criteria form to explain to the prospect your qualifying process so they know up front what it takes to move in. If you utilize this form, modify the criteria to fit your rental rate. When you are qualifying, you must stay within the fair housing laws.

Step 2: Show the property. Be sure to show the prospect all of your rental home's amenities, such as washer/dryer hookups and large closets.

Step 3: If your prospect is interested in leasing your rental property and feels confident they will qualify, your next step is to complete an application. This form is very important. Why, you ask? Because this form is the cornerstone of the tenant's file. For example, if you need to evict a resident you will need this application, along with a lease, to begin the eviction process. The application is also needed to report money owed to a collection agency. This form will serve many purposes, so be sure it is filled out completely and legibly.

Step 4: Be sure to collect your application fee! The application fee should be adequate to cover your costs of either using an agency to qualify your prospects for you, or to cover the cost of a credit check and your time. We offer tenant screening services through our website, www .landlordacademy.com.

Step 5: At this point you will also want to collect a security deposit. Explain to your prospect that the security deposit will be refundable for seventy-two hours. If their application is not approved, their deposit will be refunded, but not their application fee.

Step 6: You will now proceed to the tenant screening process. Using our tenant screening, you can now approve the prospect on the spot. This is essential to closing the deal, as if they leave, they may continue looking at other rentals and decide on another unit.

SECTION 5: THE APPROVAL PROCESS

Finding the "Blue-Chip Tenant" and Putting a Stop to the Majority of Landlord-Tenant Problems

It never fails that when the Academy holds one of its free online roundtable discussions for land-lords/property managers (by creating a profile on the website you can participate in many group forums), some of the most frequent complaints are:

"My tenant never pays on time"; "My tenant never follows the rules"; and "My tenant treats my rental like it's a barn, nightclub, or some hole-in-the-wall tavern."

Some of the More Serious Problems Associated with Not Properly Screening Your Tenants

So many landlords fall short in conducting proper criminal background checks on prospective tenants. Many landlords unknowingly move tenants into their rental units who have criminal records or are sexual predators. In 1996, Congress directed the Department of Justice to maintain a database of sex offenders. It also required the states to enact public notification laws. REMEMBER: IT IS CRUCIAL THAT YOU CONDUCT A COMPREHENSIVE SCREENING OF YOUR TENANT THAT INCLUDES A CRIMINAL BACKGROUND CHECK AND SEXUAL PREDATOR CHECK. This allows you, as a landlord, to screen your prospective tenant to see whether they are in one of these sexual predator databases. By getting the right tenant into your rental in the first place, you may decrease criminal activity you are experiencing on your property by half.

What Should a Landlord Check in a Prospective Tenant's Background?

Thorough tenant screening includes checking all prospective tenants' credit history. By law, prospects must be made aware that a consumer report will be requested. The tenant must sign a form giving the landlord permission to perform the credit search. The tenant screening should be performed after you have shown the rental unit to the prospective tenant and the prospect determines that he or she is ready to move forward. The prospect should complete an application that states they give permission for you to pull their credit report and perform a background check. A good tip to keep in mind is to make small talk with the prospect while going through the application process. Does the prospect have trouble answering simple questions or misrepresent very easy facts? Make sure your application contains a provision stating that an applicant will be rejected or tenancy terminated if the information presented is falsified. This gives you a valid way out if the prospect lied on their application.

Here are some other key items that should be checked when renting to a prospective tenant:

1. Retail credit file
2. Statewide eviction search
3. Statewide criminal check
4. Rental collection search
5. Employment verification

A Quick and Easy Way to Help Weed Out Undesirable and Dishonest Tenants

Have written rental criteria, or "qualifying criteria," that lists your approval criteria. For example, it may say that you require a tenant to have two times the monthly rent in income and that you do not allow anyone with a felony criminal record to rent from you. Be careful that your criteria does not violate any fair housing laws. Post this where it can be seen while you show the rental unit. This will help deter undesirable or dishonest tenants. Many will see your criteria and know that when you perform your tenant screening they will not be approved. They will not waste your time or their money running an application. We recommend that you go over the qualifying criteria on the telephone briefly when you schedule showing appointments so you do not waste your time meeting an unqualified prospect.

Your criteria can include:

1. A completed application
2. Up-front security deposit payment
3. Verifiable employment history
4. Verifiable income
5. At least two pieces of identification, including one government-issued photo ID

It is also a good idea to post reasons for denial:

1. Poor credit history
2. Falsified information given
3. Poor employment history
4. Poor rental history, which may include reports of disturbances, damages, failure to give proper vacating notice, failure to pay rent timely, or illegal activity
5. Criminal history that would be considered a very serious threat to the landlord's property or the current tenants or neighbors
6. Failure to meet income requirements

Making Sure you Comply with the Fair Housing Law

Whatever screening procedures you use, be sure to use them the same way for each and every prospect to avoid charges of discrimination. Use a fair process and apply it consistently and equally to all prospects.

Making Sure you Comply with the Fair Credit Reporting Act

By law you must also provide your prospect with an adverse action letter if you deny their application. This is a letter stating what credit agency you used to access their credit report and information on how they can obtain a copy of their credit report.

It Only Takes a Few Minutes and Won't Cost the Landlord a Thing!

These days, with technology, performing a tenant screening only takes a few minutes when using a reputable tenant screening company. REMEMBER, THE PROSPECT PAYS FOR THE APPLICATION, so it doesn't cost the landlord anything! So there is *no* excuse for not performing a proper tenant screening.

🖵 TIPS: Technology Hack 🖵

We have partnered with SmartMove by TransUnion to provide the best in tenant screening. Reference the tools section of the website to set up your free account. Screening is done directly through e-mail between TransUnion and the tenant—limiting tenant screening risk to the property management company. It takes minutes to set up and the completed reports are sent to you within minutes of tenant completion, with 24/7 access.

Step 1: Log onto www.landlordacademy.mysmartmove.com and perform your tenant screening. This service will:

- Search credit history
- Search criminal history
- Search eviction history
- Search rental history
- Search rental collection
- Verify employment
- Perform out-of-state searches

Step 2: If an application is not approved, provide a tenant rejection letter.
Step 3: If an application is a marginal risk, you can increase the required deposit or require

Fair Housing Law

Legal Reasons to Possibly Reject an Applicant

The following are several legal reasons you can reject an applicant (check with state and local laws for jurisdiction-specific laws):

- Poor credit history and/or income
- Poor references from previous landlords
- A record of evictions and civil lawsuits
- A criminal conviction for drug trafficking, distribution, or manufacture is specifically excluded from protection under the Fair Housing Act. However, some argue that past addiction to drugs is considered a disability under the Fair Housing Amendments Act.
- Incomplete or inaccurate rental application
- Inability to comply with the terms of the lease, such as a security deposit or the length of the lease
- Pets (unless a "reasonable accommodation" is necessary for a person with a disability)

first and last month's rent to limit your risk. Be sure to put in writing why you increased the deposit and have the tenant sign.

Step 4: If applicant is approved:

1. Complete a move-in cost sheet to explain all of the up-front costs of moving in. This form is essential to avoid any confusion on move-in day about any monies due.
2. Have them sign the lease right away. Until they actually sign the lease, all they have to lose is their security deposit if they decide to back out. Once they sign the lease, termination fees would also apply if they back out. In this day and age of a free month's rent and move-in specials, this is a necessary reinforcement. Not all leases have the language to support this technique, but The Landlord Property Management Academy™ does.

The day they sign the lease and the day that the lease term begins do not have to be the same day!

TIPS: Use Money Orders!

Be sure to explain that all money for move-in should be paid by certified check or money order!

This will protect you by avoiding the possibility of moving a tenant in with a bad check. I could tell you a story or two about tenants moving in with bad checks and landlords having to pay hundreds of dollars to evict them. See, once you move a tenant in, you must evict them, even if their check was bad. You can avoid this situation by requiring a money order or certified check on move-in day.

Step 5: Schedule a day and time for your new tenant to meet you to obtain the keys and sign any other paperwork. Schedule this meeting at the property, as you will need to complete a walk-through. (This is discussed in our next phase.)

FAIR HOUSING LAW FAIR CREDIT REPORTING ACT

If you check an applicant's credit history during your application process, which we strongly recommend, you must do so in a manner that complies with the Fair Credit Reporting Act. Our system operates within the law; therefore, we do not recommend changing or modifying Landlording 101™'s application process. If you want more details on the laws, contact the Department of Housing and Urban Development (HUD) or an attorney.

The main components of the Fair Credit Reporting Act are:

- Regulation of reports obtained from consumer reporting agencies on employees and applicants
- Properly handling the denial of an application
- Application of the law to all employers without consideration of size
- Enforcement of compliance by the Federal Trade Commission

In order to comply with the law:

- Inform applicants you will be requesting a consumer report
- Have your applicant sign an authorization for you to perform a credit search
- If an applicant is rejected, you must notify them in writing of their right to obtain a copy of their credit report. You must give them the name and address of the credit bureau that provided the report.
- Always keep a copy of your records and correspondence on file in case you need to prove you complied with the law.

How you inform a rejected applicant (due to their credit report) must comply with the law also. Be sure you do not change the tenant rejection letter we have supplied. It includes necessary items such as:

- The name, address, and phone number of the credit bureau you used
- An explanation that the rejection decision was not made by the credit bureau. Therefore, they cannot supply a reason for the rejection. They can only provide a copy of the credit report.
- Notification of the rejected applicant's right to obtain a free copy of their credit report if they request it within sixty days
- Notification that the rejected applicant can dispute the accuracy of the report as provided in Section 1681 of the Fair Credit Reporting Act

Disclaimer: Please be advised that certain laws and/or regulations vary from state to state. Accordingly, it is imperative that you thoroughly review any and all such laws and regulations and the impact of the same on your ongoing business activities. This manual is designed solely for informational purposes and is not intended and shall not be deemed to offer or provide legal (or other) advice or guidance. The Landlord Property Management Academy makes no representations or warranties that the procedures covered in this course comply with any laws, rules, or regulations, which may exist in or be applicable to your jurisdiction.

Tips for Using the Operations Manual Template

Whether or not you use our template, we recommend you use a system to operate your property management company.

For free examples of common fair-housing violations that are pertinent to property managers, please visit the blog section of the website.

💻 TIPS: Technology Hack 💻

Using technology:

Step 1: Upload all forms into your cloud-based storage platform, such as box.com.

Step 2: Download your tablet document-signing app, such as Sign Easy.

These apps and cloud-based storage platforms allow a landlord and property manager to save both time and money.

STATEMENT OF QUALIFYING CRITERIA

Thank you for visiting and applying.

To assure our neighbors of a well-maintained community, as well as enjoyable neighbors, we require that all prospective residents meet the following qualifying criteria when completing the rental application:

Applicant must be employed or have verification of subsidized housing assistance sufficient to satisfy housing expense. We require monthly gross income to be at least three times the monthly rental rate. If housing payment is subsidized, see requirements below. If income from employment is the primary source of income, a minimum of six months at the same place of employment must be verified. Self-employment will require the applicant's previous year's tax return as income verification. Income other than wages from employment such as tips, commissions, school subsidies, or allowances from parents will require notarized verification. An applicant who is not currently employed must provide proof of funds (current bank statement), which will equal the full term of the lease agreement.

Subsidized voucher holder:

- Valid and current RTA
- Provide counselor's contact information

Applicant must have a minimum of one-year verifiable rental history. Verifiable rental history for a period of at least twelve months, in which all the lease terms have been satisfactorily fulfilled, is required. Negative rental history, eviction, or outstanding monies owed to a previous landlord are unacceptable. If applicant owned a home, applicant must furnish all mortgage information. If applicant has no prior verifiable rental history, an additional security deposit up to a full month's rent will be required.

Applicant must physically reside in the apartment for which they are applying. Applicant must live in the rental unit and must disclose all persons who will be occupying the unit. All persons under the age of twenty-one are subject to background checks prior to occupancy. All persons eighteen years of age or older must be a leaseholder and qualify for the unit with the applicant.

Credit history for a two-year period prior to this application will be evaluated. No credit history as well as discharged bankruptcies is acceptable. Negative credit history, other than not fulfilling terms of a lease contract, will be considered provided there are more positive accounts than negative accounts. More than 30 percent of applicant's credit accounts showing negative remarks is unacceptable.

A criminal background check will be done on all applicants and any occupant eighteen years of age or older. No felony convictions within the past five years will be accepted. No misdemeanor convictions against persons or property, prostitution, or drug-related offenses will be accepted.

If rental property is a single-family dwelling or single unit, landlord reserves the right to ask for a security deposit equal to one month's rent and first and last month's rent in advance.

If you are inquiring about an apartment or duplex, occupancy limits have been established per unit size. Maximum number of persons allowed is as follows with no more than three unrelated adults per apartment or duplex in either a two- or three-bedroom floor plan:

Studio/Efficiency: no more than two persons
One-Bedroom: no more than two persons
Two-Bedroom: no more than four persons
Three-Bedroom: no more than six persons

In order to view a rental home you must show a form of identification. Your driver's license or an alternate second form of identification will be photocopied. Please have identification with you.

We do business in accordance with the Federal Fair Housing Law. We do not discriminate against any person because of race, color, religion, sex, national origin, familial status, or disability.

I have read and understand the above qualifying criteria.

Note: False information given on an application will be grounds for rejection of the application.

Applicant _____ Date _____

Applicant _____ Date _____

VACATION RENTALS: WHAT TAXES DOES THE OWNER NEED TO PAY?

Here is the brass tacks of it all. The rent is not the only thing that is taxable. Most states' Department of Revenue will view the *total* amount charged to the seasonal renter as taxable. Many seasonal agreements spell out the rent as well as cleaning charges. What property managers must realize is that the cleaning charge is taxable as well. This is a common mistake. Below is a list of other items that owners and property managers often overlook but need to realize is taxable.

Taxable Items

The following are some of the charges the DOR has stated are taxable, but this is not an all-inclusive list. You may have other charges that also could be considered by the DOR as taxable. If in doubt, err on the safe side and charge the tax.

1. *The base rent:* This is the most obvious charge.
2. *Cleaning:* Simply add the cleaning charge to the bill. The DOR is fully aware of the lack of knowledge of the property managers.

3. *Electricity:* Any amount paid by the tenant for electricity is taxable. In many but not all seasonal rentals, the electric is included in the rent, especially in weekly rentals. Sometimes, though, the tenant does pay the electric in full or an amount over and above a particular amount set by the landlord.
4. *Parking:* Some condominiums that allow seasonal rentals charge additional vehicle fees or parking fees, and these are taxable.
5. *Other miscellaneous charges:* security, garbage pickup, furniture rental, lifeguard, clubhouse use. If these amounts are extra, and the tenant must pay for them, the amounts are taxable.

Other potentially taxable items:

1. *Application fee:* If an application fee is required, this fee may also be subject to the tax.
2. *Condo approval fee:* Although the law is unclear about this item, this may be taxable.

Situational Exceptions

Most, but not all seasonal rentals, are subject to taxation. Some exceptions are carved out but not frequently encountered. A seasonal rental to a full-time college student is exempt from taxation. Rentals to federal employees are exempted if they are performing work-related duties. For example, FEMA employees need a place to rent on a short-term basis when they are responding to major storms, like flash floods and earthquakes. Military personnel traveling under military orders and diplomats are also exempt. It is the responsibility of the lessor to obtain all the necessary documentation from the tenant before any exemption should be given. Always check with your accountant or attorney if you are unsure of being in compliance.

Inspect What You Expect

You will want to make sure your lease or reservation agreement specifically outlines the taxable amounts. If a tenant refuses to pay, refer them to the law. If the reservation agreement or guest agreement does not properly explain that the sales tax is the responsibility of the guest, and they refuse to pay, the owner may have to pay the amount due. It is highly recommended to visit your state's DOR website to review their sales and use tax guide for vacation and transient rentals.

MOVING YOUR TENANT IN

SECTION 1: PRIOR TO YOUR MOVE-IN MEETING

You will want to prepare your paperwork prior to meeting with your tenant.

Step 1: Complete the lease. Most of us know the definition of a lease. It is a contract between the landlord and the tenant that spells out the terms and conditions of the tenancy. With that said, my goal is for you, the property manager, to be able to distinguish between a well-written lease and a poorly written lease. Our survival as landlords depends on it. A lease is one of the most important lines of defense your investment has.

Again, when dealing with a vacation rental, you DO NOT have a landlord-tenant relationship. You have a property manager–guest relationship. You are dealing with short-term agreements, not long-term leases. It is best practice to use terms such as guest (instead of tenant) and check-in/checkout policy (instead of lease agreement). This procedure should be close to the experience of checking in and out of a hotel.

UNDERSTANDING THE IMPORTANCE OF THE LEASE

The lease is the first line of defense that your investment has. This contract will be put to the test on occasion throughout a tenant's lease term. So it's imperative that you reflect on this section until the terms used become second nature.

Lease Breakdown

Understanding in advance these key elements can identify a well-written lease. The lease should:

- Recognize all parties involved
- Use the correct legal names
- Recognize all occupants who are of legal age and require their signatures

(Check with your local landlord-tenant attorney. This is not required in all states.)

- State the duration of lease term, beginning date, lease date, and expiration date
- State required methods of payments (i.e., check, certified check, or money order)
- State rental amount
- State complete address, rental unit number, street address, city, state, and zip code
- Give very detailed description of the premises that will be under lease contract
- Give the name of managing agent or owner and community name, if any
- State payment terms:
  - Underline when the rent is due and the amount of any late fees that are assessed
  - Where payments are to be made
- Spell out clearly the returned check policy
- State causes for any legal action
- State acceptable use of premises
- State termination procedure and requirements for submitting notice to vacate
- Give holdover tenant language
- State terms and conditions of rental increase
- Contain abandonment language
- Contain radon gas language (if applicable in your state)

Note: It is also common to include mold language in your lease or in an addendum. Without it you might be asking for a lawsuit!

The lease should also identify other key issues such as:

- Who's responsible for certain maintenance issues
- Condition of premises
- Landlord or landlord's agent's right of access
- Renter's insurance
- Subletting policy
- Any pet policies or procedures
- Utilities
- Security deposit
- Parking

(Always check with a local landlord-tenant attorney to see what other language your state statutes indicate should be in your lease. You want to add any language your law allows to protect yourself in the future!)

Hopefully you now have a basic understanding of not only the definition of a lease but, more important, the key components that make up a well-written lease.

TIPS: Accepting Cash Payments

Cash is a legal, accepted method of payment. Not accepting the cash could negate the resident's rent responsibility for that month. However, cash is not recommended as a source of payment. For your safety and the safety of your staff, you should use caution when accepting cash. Try to deposit the cash in the bank as soon as possible.

TIPS: Using the Proper Lease

The lease is your first line of defense. Using a well-written lease is critical. You may have tenants already on a lease. As soon as their lease term ends, have them sign the lease in this manual. This lease was written exclusively for the PROFESSIONAL PROPERTY MANAGEMENT™ Operations Manual by Bryan M. Chavis and a premier Florida eviction attorney. Many leases you get from Realtors or online are not Florida-specific and have lots of loopholes. We highly recommend you visit the U.S. legal document section of our website to find your state-specific lease.

TIPS: Late Fees

Late fees should be addressed in your lease. You should have your tenant initial by your late-fee charge. I recommend charging at least $50 as a late fee. Some like to charge $50 after the grace period expires and $2 a day every day after until the rent is paid and late fees are paid in full. Many judges have ruled this excessive. Also remember, you can only charge late fees that are indicated in your lease. So again, it is important to have a well-written lease like the one in this manual.

Step 2: Complete addendums.

Addendums are key in pointing out the rules and regulations to be enforced by the owner, management, or agent. They allow you to add customizations to the lease that pertain to your property and/or the specific rules you wish to be enforced. A common addendum is a pet addendum.

We have included important addendums we recommend you use in our system. If you feel you need to address other specific areas of concern, you can obtain additional addendums from an eviction attorney.

Step 3: Gather and organize the rest of your move-in forms.

SECTION 2: MEETING WITH YOUR TENANT FOR MOVE-IN

Step 1: When your tenant arrives for their move-in meeting, if they have not already signed the lease as we recommended, review the lease with them and have them sign it now. They should sign their name exactly as it appears on the lease contract.

Step 2: Review any addendums with them and have them sign those also.

Step 3: Review the rules and regulations form. This form should contain general rules you want followed.

Step 4: Collect your first month's rent. (If you are requiring last month's rent, collect that also.) Again, be sure to collect a money order or cashier's check.

TIPS: Separate Accounts for Security Deposit

You should open two separate bank accounts for depositing your security deposits and your rent.

A security deposit is not your money. You cannot spend it. The IRS likes to see that the funds are *not* commingled. This is a must for security deposits. I recommend you use a bank that returns canceled checks to help you with maintaining your records.

STUDY SESSION: Understanding Security Deposits

A diligent landlord/property manager will always seek to collect a security deposit for various reasons. For example, collecting a deposit as soon as possible can help ensure that a prospective tenant will return after a visit to your property. It deters the prospect from looking at other rental properties. Another important reason is just as the name implies. The deposit is the landlord's/property manager's security to help ensure the lease contract is fulfilled. The deposit can help to ensure there is money available in case of damages left by the tenant after he or she moves out. You can also require an extra deposit if the prospective tenant's rental or credit history has some discrepancies.

Many landlords/property managers like to charge a pet deposit. Remember, deposit implies refundable. So if your intent is to keep the money paid by a tenant for having a pet, then call it a "pet fee," not a pet deposit. The term "nonrefundable deposit" is an oxymoron and should not be used.

Collecting Procedures for a Security Deposit

A landlord/property manager must not collect a deposit from more than one applicant at a time for the same rental unit. It is good practice to collect other applications for the same unit in case the first applicant does not qualify, but do not collect more than one deposit. The second applicant should be informed that there is someone ahead of them and if that applicant does not take the rental unit, then they will be next in line to be considered.

Last Month's Rent

Problems can occur when allowing a tenant to apply their security deposit to their last month's rent because the condition in which the rental unit will be left is unknown. Current market conditions may not call for the security deposit to be equal to current rental rates or the cost of repair. You could have applied the security deposit for last month's rent and now have nothing left to cover damages.

If a tenant chooses not to pay last month's rent and requests you use their security deposit instead, you should treat this as rent nonpayment. The landlord/property manager should follow the steps in this operations manual for nonpayment of rent. If after receiving the proper notice the tenant still has not paid, then you must follow the necessary legal steps to file for an eviction.

Step 5: Walk through the unit and inspect its condition with your tenant. Complete the move-in/move-out inspection report. This form should be used twice. The first time is when the tenant moves in. Walk through the unit with the tenant, having them point out any damage or abnormalities. List each noted area or item on the move-in/move-out inspection report.

Example: If an appliance has chipped paint prior to move-in, note the chipped paint on the form. Be detailed and accurate to differentiate the old damage from any new damage. Clearly explain to the tenant that they will not be charged when they move out for any damage noted on this form. Explain to them the importance of walking through the unit and noting any damages to avoid being charged for damages they did not do.

The second time this form is used is during move-out, which we will discuss later.

TIPS: Move-in/Move-out Pictures

You and your nice new tenant will surely differ in your recollections of the condition of the rental property as it was when they moved in compared with how it is when they finally move out. You should have a written and photographic record of both conditions.

Step 6: Give your tenant a set of keys to their unit and any other keys, such as for the pool area, gate, and/or storage.

Step 7: Make sure you save all documents in your cloud-based storage. Once it is saved into your system, be sure to send a copy to your new tenant via e-mail. Your cloud-based storage platform should allow for you to easily e-mail your tenant all signed documents.

SECTION 3: AFTER THE MOVE-IN MEETING

Step 1: Save all documents in your tenant's file.

Step 2: Note in your file any notable discussions you had with your tenant.

TIPS: Follow Up with Tenant

Calendar a reminder for yourself a week out to check in with your tenant. This is simply a phone call to your tenant to ask how they are enjoying their new home.

Ask them if they have any questions about living there. This simple act can clear up any confusion and avoid future tenant problems caused by simple misunderstanding.

Again, note in your tenant's file anything particular you discussed. Make a practice of always noting discussions involving the rules or anything notable. This documentation can prove valuable in the future if a dispute arises.

DURING YOUR TENANT'S RESIDENCY

During a lease term, certain scenarios may occur that you may have questions about. Some of the most common are addressed below.

If you have further questions or are uncertain about a legal aspect of landlording, please consult a landlord-tenant or eviction attorney.

SECTION 1: LATE RENT

Rent Collection

Landlording/property management is a very interpersonal job. You have to be able to work with many different types of individuals and wear many different hats day to day. One of the most uncomfortable tenant conversations you will have is about late rent. Many regret or just flat-out refuse to deal with this subject. Obviously, this is an unrealistic approach to take, considering rent is the major source of income for rental property. Rental income usually pays the mortgage on the property. You should deal with the subject of late rent head-on.

Rent collection will be one of your most important tasks. A very important tool to have is a well-written lease contract that will clearly spell out the terms and the conditions of the rental payments within the lease contract.

1. Be very persistent. Always remind a tenant when they have not paid rent.
2. Follow your procedure to help provide consistency.

Typically, a landlord/property manager will choose to use a computer software program to assist with keeping all the tenants' account ledgers in order. Through software, landlords/property managers gain the ability to better manage the property. In addition, the software program will offer financial controls as well as valuable reporting functions. In a nutshell, property management software provides an easy avenue for obtaining a high-quality look and feel to your business.

One of the most important reports you should review often will be the delinquency report. The delinquency report will list individually all the tenants who are behind on their rent or who have unsettled balances. *(The delinquency report should be reviewed no less than three times a month.)*

What Is a Delinquency Report?

A delinquency report will quickly tell the property manager or landlord which tenant(s) is in arrears with their rent and any other balances due. It is common to run a delinquency report on the sixth, fifteenth, and twentieth of the month. After you deliver your three-day notices and they expire, you should evaluate a delinquency report to see who has still not paid rent. Then follow these steps:

Step 1: Pull all delinquent files.
Step 2: Gather application, lease, and three-day notice.
Step 3: Send file to your eviction attorney.

It is recommended that the landlord or property manager fully understand how to pull a delinquency report from their property management software and/or how to create a delinquency report from scratch.

Tip: Most jurisdictions have not caught up legally to current technology. Notices need to be physically placed. Do not text or e-mail notices. It is a good idea to document posting of the notice by taking a picture and saving it. This helps avoid problems later if the tenant says it was not posted.

Another report commonly used by a landlord/property manager is the rent roll. The rent roll is a very detailed record of occupancy and rent collection activity. It should include any and all addresses, each tenant's move-in date, lease expiration date, current rental rate, and the current tenant balance for the current month. This report will typically be used as the foundation that will support all other types of reports associated with the rental property.

Rent is due on the day of the month specifically stated in your lease, usually the first day of each month. Most landlords give a three- to five-day grace period. This means rent can be paid no later than the third or fifth day of the month before late fees are applied and a **three-day notice** is delivered. After the grace period is over, rent and the late fee must be paid in the form of a money order or certified check. A personal check is no longer acceptable.

Example: If your grace period expires on the fifth day of the month, the three-day notice is delivered on the sixth. Be sure to read the "rights and wrongs of the three-day notice" in the legal section of this manual.

Nonpayment of Rent Notice Rules

A three-day notice is a form required to be delivered prior to any legal action taken for the tenant not paying rent.

Keep in mind the three-day notice excludes the date of delivery, Saturdays, Sundays, and legal holidays from calculation of the notice expiration date.

Although a three-day notice is not hard to fill out, this form is the most abused.

The amount owed should be the rent only, not any late fees, *unless your lease specifies you can include late fees as "additional rent."* The lease in this manual does provide this language.

Make sure you count a full three days, again excluding the date of delivery, Saturdays, Sundays, and legal holidays, and then write the appropriate expiration date on the form.

Step 1: Fill out a three-day notice. This form should be completed and delivered on the first day the grace period expires.

Step 2: Deliver the three-day notice by placing it on the delinquent tenant's door. If the tenant is not home, mark the notice to indicate how it was delivered on the tenant's copy and on your file copy.

Step 3: If three days pass and rent has not been paid, begin the eviction process immediately. Eviction is a specific legal process with particular rules that must be followed exactly and in the proper sequence. The wrong move can turn the tables in your tenant's favor. A conservative estimate for a timely eviction—from filing suit to physical removal of your tenant—is three to four weeks.

We always recommend the use of an eviction attorney.

SECTION 2: ACCEPTING PARTIAL RENT

Accepting partial rent is a practice commonly used by a landlord or property manager. The procedure is when a resident only pays part of the rent. The property manager will accept the partial payment while issuing another three-day notice for the remaining balance. This three-day notice should be issued on the spot, as soon as partial rent is accepted.

WARNING

Be careful of accepting partial rent. The reason is that the tenant could use that extra three days the notice gives them to file for bankruptcy. If a tenant files for bankruptcy, the property manager must stop all attempts to collect rent. A tenant filing for bankruptcy will also stop an eviction cold.

If your tenant does file for bankruptcy, call your attorney, who will check with the federal bankruptcy court to see whether a bankruptcy has actually been filed. The attorney will then prepare a motion to obtain relief from the automatic stay of bankruptcy. You must petition the bankruptcy court to allow the stay to be lifted so that the landlord or property manager can collect the debt or continue to move forward with the eviction. This process can typically take thirty to forty-five days, depending on how the tenant files for bankruptcy. At most it could take up to sixty days.

All this quickly adds up to lost money and a very unhappy owner, and we can afford neither! Something to think about next time you find yourself accepting partial rent.

SECTION 3: HANDLING RETURNED CHECKS

If a resident has a returned check, that tenant's account ledger should be considered unpaid and delinquent. Follow the steps in section 1 regarding late rent.

Follow these steps to address the NSF check:

Step 1: Send a **dishonored check notice** to the tenant and include a three-day notice ASAP. This will inform the tenant of their delinquency.

Step 2: Make a copy of the **dishonored check notice** and a copy of the notification received from the bank alerting you of the NSF. Also make a copy of the check. Place in your tenant's file.

Step 3: Update the tenant's account ledger either manually or in your property management software. Add your NSF charge as indicated in your lease. It is very important you update the account ledger immediately upon receiving the NSF notice.

Step 4: Add tenant's name, address, check amount, and check number to your monthly NSF log. Use this log to follow up and make sure all NSF checks are collected.

SECTION 4: TENANTS WHO BREAK THE RULES

What If a Tenant Breaks the Rules?

NOTE: When serving notices or visiting tenants' rental homes it's not a bad idea to take pictures of you serving the notices or even videotape the process, for the property manager's protection.

Step 1: Issue a **disturbance notice**. Be detailed in your description of the disturbance.

Step 2: Deliver the disturbance notice by placing it on the tenant's door or delivering it directly to the tenant.

Step 3: Be sure to note any subsequent conversations and/or correspondence in your tenant's file.

Step 4: If a tenant continues to break the rules, issue a **seven-day notice to cure**. Be very detailed with the subject matter on the notice.

Step 5: Deliver the seven-day notice by placing it on the tenant's door or delivering it directly to the tenant.

TIPS: Proper Names on a Notice

Be certain that the name you put on any notice is the same name that appears on the lease. Also, if more than one name appears on the lease, be sure to put all the names on the notice.

Step 6: Be sure to note any subsequent conversations and/or correspondence in your tenant's file. Technology can drastically reduce liability and risk with proper documentation. Refer to the website for more information on what technology to use and how it works.

Step 7: If a tenant continues to break the rules after the seven-day notice expires, you have the legal right to send a **seven-day notice to terminate lease**.

STUDY SESSION: Using the Proper Notice

Below are suggested examples of when to use certain notices. If you have a question about the appropriate notice to use, you should consult a landlord-tenant eviction attorney.

Disturbance Notice:
- Use for disturbances, loud music, arguing, parties, etc.

Seven-Day Notice to Cure:
- Continued, documented disturbances
- Illegal occupant (a person moved in who is not on the lease)
- Illegal pet
- Uncleanliness
- Damages

Seven-Day Notice to Vacate:
- Severe continued, documented disturbances
- Illegal activity
- Extensive damages

SECTION 5: GAINING ENTRY TO A TENANT'S RENTAL UNIT

Many states have laws in place requiring the landlord/property manager to send a notice alerting the tenant of the landlord's/property manager's intent to enter the rental unit for a nonemergency reason. Required or not, it is good tenant relation practice to always provide a notice for entry for a nonemergency reason.

You will always have the right to enter without the permission of the tenant for an emergency. Cases where there is not sufficient time to alert the tenant of an emergency include:

- Fire or smoke coming from the doors and windows
- Excessive water leaking out of doors, windows, floors, walls, or ceilings
- Loud screaming
- A smell of natural gas
- No answer at door or not hearing from a tenant for an unusually long period of time

TIPS for Notifying Tenant

- Always provide the tenant with a written notification, a **notice of intent to enter**
- Give the tenant as much notice as possible. (Check with your local landlord-tenant attorney for any required compliance.)
- Try to enter the unit while the tenant is home, to avoid any claims of theft.
- Do not force your way into the tenant's home if there are no emergencies.
- Follow all entry procedures in your operations manual to provide consistency.
- Follow your operations manual for dealing with maintenance issues. Always have the maintenance technician leave the "work performed" letter behind notifying the tenant that they were there and of the work that was performed. (*Review Phase 4: Maintenance for more detail about the work order forms that should be used.*)

SECTION 6: RENT COLLECTION

Knowing that rent is due on the first, with a grace period through the fifth day of the month (or however you choose to set up your grace period), you should collect all rent checks by the last day of your grace period.

Step 1: Document all rent checks and money orders used to pay rent. Use your camera or a scanning app and create a backup.

Step 2: Post your checks in a ledger to reflect which tenant has paid rent. If you do not have property management software, you should post your checks or money orders in a program that will keep track of and balance your books.

Step 3: Deposit checks and money orders as soon as possible. Keep these backup documents safe. In the event of a major technology failure or data loss, you need to fall back on them and avoid catastrophe.

TIPS: Collecting Cash

I recommend you avoid accepting cash. One reason is for safety. Also, cash is easy to misplace.

TIPS: Easy-to-Use System

Make sure you create an easy-to-use system or take advantage of using property management software for keeping track of your rent checks. If you follow the system above, you should be on your way.

MAINTENANCE: READYING A UNIT, REPAIRS, AND PREVENTIVE MAINTENANCE

This phase contains a general overview of maintenance and some common forms you will need. For a more comprehensive maintenance guide, including troubleshooting and tips for working with a maintenance tech or contractor, visit the members section of our website, www.landlordacademy.com.

SECTION 1: PREPARING A RENTAL UNIT FOR OCCUPANCY

Your focus at this point is to fix up, paint, and clean the unit so you can lease it to a new tenant. Basically, you want to dress up the rental unit and make it attractive so that a good prospect will want to rent it from you and pay the rental price you are requesting.

Keep in mind that time is of the essence. You want to rent your unit as soon as possible!

TIPS: Readying the Unit

When readying your unit to show to potential tenants, always play to the senses. This includes sight and smell. A visually attractive unit that smells fresh and clean will make a great impression.

Step 1: The following is a basic checklist for readying your unit:
- Clean all appliances.
- Clean cabinets, inside and outside.
- Remove all nonadhesive shelf paper.
- Clean the showers and bathtubs.
- Clean all sinks.
- Clean toilets.
- Clean medicine cabinet, inside and out.
- Clean mirrors.

- Dust miniblinds.
- Change A/C filter.

In short, clean and dust everything! Leave no stone unturned.

Step 2: Remove any items left in the unit from the last tenant. No new tenant wants to be reminded that someone else lived there. They want to feel as if this is their home. Be sure to check top shelves and closets.

Step 3: Clean carpets!

Step 4: Touch up paint if necessary.

For a comprehensive make-ready checklist visit the members section of our website, www.landlordacademy.com.

SECTION 2: REPAIRS

Tenants renting a house will expect less maintenance services than apartment tenants. They will tend to do more things for themselves, rather than bothering the landlord or owner. However, no matter what type of property you are renting, you will be involved and responsible for certain repairs.

Step 1: Inform your tenant of whom they should contact if they need something repaired and the phone number to contact them at. (If this is an office, be sure to give them a contact and number for emergency repairs that may need to be done at night, on weekends, or on holidays.)

　　You should have informed your tenant during your first walk-through of the residence of certain components that may be important during an emergency, such as:

- Where the water shut-off valve is
- Where the main breaker is
- Where the hot-water tank is and how to detect problems with the components

Step 2: Set clear expectations from the beginning with your tenant on how long a repair will take and your response time.

Step 3: When a tenant does call with maintenance needs, always fill out a **work order**. Once it is completed, place a copy in the tenant's file. Place a second copy in a file containing only work orders. This second file will help you forecast when your property will need major repairs and renovations by tracking the types of repairs that are being made.

SECTION 3: PREVENTIVE MAINTENANCE

Taking a proactive approach to preventive maintenance will save you a lot of money and time in the long run. It will also play a big part in keeping your tenants happy and increasing your tenant retention.

Basically, preventive maintenance consists of two parts. The first is setting up a schedule to replace certain items in your rental units to prevent them from wearing out and causing major (expensive) damage. Several of these items should be replaced as the seasons change to compensate for the damage that can occur from weather.

The second part of preventive maintenance is setting a schedule to routinely check certain appliances and items, to be sure they are not wearing out. Often if you catch something in its beginning stages, the repair will be much smaller, such as replacing a hose. Also, if an appliance or plumbing is leaking, repairing this early will help to prevent water damage to the walls, floors, and carpets.

We have provided a **preventive maintenance checklist**. We recommend you complete this checklist at least twice a year, once in the spring and once in the fall.

As you conduct your maintenance checks, keep track of each of your appliances and fixtures, along with their life expectancy and warranty dates. This will help you budget when you will need to spend money on new appliances and fixtures. You should create a "reserve for replacement budget." This is money set aside for replacing items as they wear out or for emergency repairs.

SECTION 4: KEY CONTROL

The key control system is very important. It is a good practice to not allow the use of master keys. Steps for key control:

Step 1: It is the property manager's or landlord's responsibility to maintain strict key control.
Step 2: All office personnel and tenants must strictly adhere to the rules of key control.
Step 3: Keys should be stored in a key cabinet. The cabinet must stay locked at all times. Only the property manager or landlord should have the key to the key cabinet and only the landlord or property manager should release the key to a fellow employee.
Step 4: Code all keys with a random code system. Do not make reference to a building or residence. Store the key code away from the key cabinet.

Step 5: Place two keys in the key cabinet for each apartment unit or residency; at move-in one key per adult should be issued. Tenants may be charged for extra keys.

Step 6: Make sure all keys are returned at move-out. The total number of keys should be documented on the notice to impose a claim on the security deposit if you are charging for not returning keys.

Step 7: Any time keys are issued to a tenant, vendor, or staff, it should be noted in a key control log located in the general area of the key cabinet. Do not allow the vendor, tenant, or employee to keep the keys overnight. All keys must be brought back by the end of the business day.

Step 8: A well-maintained key log should be kept as follows:

- Note the date the key was borrowed
- Note the name of the individual checking out the key
- Note the time the key was issued
- Note the time the key was returned

💻 TIPS: Technology Hack 💻

Smart locks enable users to grant limited access to individuals remotely, saving time and improving accountability.

APPROACHING THE END OF A LEASE TERM

SECTION 1

There is no specific law on how the landlord or property manager must deliver the notice, so here are a few recommended options:

1. Hand delivery
2. Post the notice on the door

Make sure that the lease you are using allows for this type of delivery of notices. The lease in this manual does allow either choice of delivery above.

Step 1: Landlord or property manager provides tenant written notice of approaching notice obligation period not more than forty-five days prior to the end of the lease term and not less than thirty-one days before the end of the lease term.

Step 2: A tenant is required to give a thirty-day notice in writing.

Step 3: If you receive a notice from the tenant telling you of their intent to vacate, log the thirty-day notice in the tenant's file.

Step 4: You should then immediately send a letter explaining that it was a pleasure having them as a tenant and that you wish them all the best in the future. You should also take this time to explain to them your requirements upon move-out. The letter explains in detail the condition the rental unit should be left in. It also explains your inspection procedures, lists the legal deductions you subtract from their security deposit, and tells the vacating tenant when and how their refund, if any, will be returned.

Basic Elements of a Move-Out Letter

1. Request a forwarding address.
2. Inform the tenant that any and all fixtures the tenant has permanently attached to the rental unit must be left in place. (A common example is a satellite dish.)
3. Spell out any specific cleaning requirements.
4. Also add any state law information that lets you, as the landlord/property manager, keep the deposit if the tenant did not provide a forwarding address within a certain time frame. (Note: this is only available in certain states.)

If You Choose to Renew the Lease with Your Tenant

Step 1: Forty-five to sixty days prior to the end of a tenant's lease, send your tenant a renewal form. This form will show the rental increase or the additional month-to-month charge if a tenant decides to go month to month.

Step 2: If you do not hear from your resident before thirty days prior to the end of their lease, call your tenant and ask them if their intention is to stay or to move out.

TIPS: Raising Rents

I recommend raising rents at the end of each lease term. Even if only a few dollars, it gets your tenant accustomed to the rents being raised. You should bring the rents up to market rate at this time.

To find out what market rents are in your area, do a market survey. Many find it helpful to use a tool such as Google or Rentometer.

TIPS: Minimizing Vacancy Loss

You will always want to know your tenant's intention to leave as early as possible so that you can begin finding a new tenant. This will minimize the amount of time your unit is vacant and you are incurring the cost of vacancy loss. Sending out your renewal form forty-five to sixty days prior to the end of a lease term will help you to determine your tenant's plans early on.

As the landlord, you can choose *not* to renew a tenant's lease. This is accomplished by using a nonrenewal form. This form must be sent out at least thirty days prior to the end of the lease term. (Check your lease for specific language regarding this requirement.)

SECTION 2: THE MONTH-TO-MONTH PROCESS

Step 1: In a well-written lease, month to month occurs automatically when a tenant has failed to notify you of their decision to move out or renew their lease. A tenant can also opt to go month to month at the end of their lease. Preferably the month-to-month term should be no more than ninety days.

Step 2: The first month after the lease term is over, the rent due is the new rental rate that you put on the renewal form (the market-value rent). Your lease should also state that you charge a month-to-month fee.

Step 3: If the tenant pays rent without the new rental rate and additional month-to-month fees, you should immediately send the rent back with a **three-day notice**. If you have not collected all the rent by the time the three-day notice expires, you should prepare the file for EVICTION! (Contact your eviction attorney.)

SECTION 3: MOVE-OUT

Technology now allows the process of documenting the move-out much easier. Please take the time and download one of the many apps available to you to help document the entire move-out process. You will want to:

1. Take video and photos of the condition of the unit after the tenant has moved out.
2. Save any photos and videos into the tenant's file.
3. Once all photos have been saved into the tenant's file, make sure you rename the tenant file from current to moved out.

Step 1: Upon receiving notice from a tenant of their intention to vacate, or if you notify a tenant you are not renewing their lease, you should immediately attempt to schedule a move-out meeting. During this meeting the tenant should return the keys to you, provide a forwarding address if they haven't already, pay any balance due, and conduct a move-out inspection with you.

Step 2: At the move-out meeting, use your **move-in/move out inspection form** and walk through the unit and note any damages or areas in need of repair. You will be using the same move-in/move-out inspection form you used to move the tenant in to compare the condition. Indicate any damages that were not marked present at move-in.

Example: If an appliance had chipped paint prior to move-in, that damage should be noted on the form from the move-in inspection. Be detailed and accurate to differentiate the old damage from any new damage. Clearly explain to the tenant that they will not be charged when they move out for any damage noted on this form at move-in.

You and your tenant's recollection of the condition of the rental property as it was when they moved in compared with how it is when they move out may differ, so always utilize your move-in/move-out inspection report along with pictures of the unit before and after.

TIPS: Move-Out Inspection

If possible, schedule your move-out inspection after the tenant has removed their furniture. It is easy to hide stained carpet or holes in the wall behind a sofa!

If the tenant is very hostile upon move-out and you feel they would cause a problem during the move-out inspection, then perform the inspection accompanied by a friend or staff member. Never perform a walk-through or a move-out inspection alone if you question your safety.

If a tenant will not show up for the move-out meeting, or skips out on you without notice, you can perform the move-out inspection without them. Your tenant's signature on the move-in/move-out condition form upon move-in, agreeing to the condition of your rental unit when they took possession, along with photos of the current condition, is all the evidence you need.

We recommend, if possible, going ahead and conducting the move-out inspection with your tenant to discuss any disputes then and there, rather than prolong them.

Step 3: After your meeting with your tenant ends, back at your office calculate the cost of repairing the damages reflected on the move-in/move-out inspection report.

Step 4: Prepare a **notice to impose claim on security deposit**. Be sure to show a calculation of all damage charges found in the unit. Show the deduction of these charges from the security deposit.

Step 5: Mail the notice to impose claim. You must send the notice to impose claim to either the last known address or any new address the vacating tenant provided to you. If a new address was not provided to you, then mail it to your rental unit's address, as this is the last known address you have for the tenant. Typically, they have put in a forwarding request for their mail and will still receive the notice. If you plan to deduct charges from the vacating tenant's security deposit, you must send the notice to impose claim *by certified mail*. Include a copy of the move-in/move-out inspection report in your mailing. This must be sent within thirty days, which is an extension from the fifteen days allowed by the previous law. If a refund of the security deposit or a portion of the deposit is due to the tenant, enclose a check.

The Security Deposit: What to Take and What Not to Take

The security deposit dispute is one of the most common areas of litigation in landlord-tenant law. In some states, a tenant has up to four years to sue the landlord over security deposit claims. However, after the first year the chances of that happening greatly decline. If you do find yourself in court, the best defense, in my opinion, is to be well organized by having the move-out procedure well documented. The operations manual provides you with consistency and professionalism.

Noteworthy tips for security deposit deductions are as follows:

- A fair price should be charged for repairs and replacements. Judges may rule against you if your fees cannot be substantiated or are exorbitant.
- The security deposit should not be considered a landlord or property manager's source of income. It is not *your* money.
- Do not charge a tenant for replacing an item when it can be easily repaired.
- Always take into consideration the length of the tenant's occupancy. You may find it difficult to collect money for cleaning carpet and repainting walls if the tenant lived in the unit for a period longer than one year. This may be considered normal wear and tear and not something you can charge for.
- Do not charge for conditions that were seen and noted on the move-in/move-out inspection report upon the tenant moving in.

TIPS: Using the Security Deposit for Rent

It is not recommended to allow a tenant to use the security deposit for rent payments during the tenancy. Use your other collection techniques to acquire rent payments. Applying the security deposit toward rent during the lease term will deplete the protection the deposit provides you for damage repair. A security deposit is just that: your security against repairs and damages when the tenant leaves.

General Rules of Thumb Regarding Move-Out Procedure

Ordinarily you *can* charge for:

- Replacing ruined, stained, or torn carpet
- Replacing chipped tile
- Replacing broken blinds or drapes
- Fixing damaged furniture
- Pest control for flea infestation
- Patching holes in walls

- Replacing broken doorknobs
- Replacing torn or missing window screens
- Replacing broken window glass
- Cleaning for an excessively dirty kitchen or bathroom

You typically should *not* charge for:

- Any condition present at move-in
- Replacement of an item that could be repaired

Areas of common disagreement:

- **Painting of interior walls.** The rule of thumb is that if a resident has lived in a residence for more than one year, the need for new paint is normal wear and tear and should *not* be charged for. If they have lived there for less than one year, and the walls were newly painted upon their moving in, you can charge them for painting. Either way, you *can* charge for repairing walls.
- **Cleaning of carpets.** Again, the rule of thumb is one year's occupancy. If the carpet was new upon move-in, and is stained and torn within months, you can charge the tenant. This is more than normal wear and tear. If the carpet was already worn upon move-in, you should not charge to clean it, even if it looks worse upon move-out. This is considered normal wear and tear.
- **Fixtures.** Any furniture, fixtures, or equipment that a tenant attaches to the apartment is the property of the landlord. They cannot be removed by the tenant.

In addition, do not charge a tenant for cleaning if they already paid a nonrefundable cleaning fee. You can't charge them twice.

Also, be sure to charge fair prices for repairs and replacements. This will help you avoid disputes and bad publicity. Security deposits should not be counted on as an income source. Their purpose is to cover the cost of repairs.

SECTION 4: THE ART OF THE RENTAL INCREASE

The rental increase is one of the most important processes a landlord/property manager will have to master. Without periodic rental increases a rental property could stand to lose a considerable amount of cash flow.

A well-thought-out rental increase plan can help with key issues such as:

- The rising cost of doing business
- Recovering any losses suffered by the investment
- Adding additional amenities
- Upgrading and fixing any needed repairs on the rental property

Being able to raise the rent is one of the things that make rental property a solid investment. It's a good hedge against inflation.

There has been a lot written on how and when you tell the tenant that the rent they are currently paying will be increased. Landlords/property managers have been known to offer such things as new microwaves, TVs, ceiling fans, and other items at the end of a lease term to incentivize the tenant to renew their lease. The end of the lease term is also when the rent is usually increased, so these incentives are thought to help sugarcoat the rent raise. It has been my personal experience that tenants respond more positively to an increase in rent when they have been treated with respect and the landlord/property manager has maintained their rental property. In 2001, I conducted a poll of tenants whose leases were coming up for renewal and whose current rents were to be raised. My staff and myself were pretty shocked when we found out that the reason most tenants decided to renew their leases was not that they would get a free microwave or a free TV, but that, as most tenants put it, our management was professional and they actually felt that they mattered to our staff. Moreover, the study also showed that our attention to detail and timing with respect to maintenance requests was a huge deciding factor that helped persuade a tenant to renew their lease. In the highly competitive rental market, maintaining high levels of tenant satisfaction is one way to increase retention. If you're a numbers person, reducing the number of units that have to be "made-ready" for another tenant will have a direct positive effect on the net operating income (NOI). For the owner, this translates to return on investment.

Simple Techniques Used to Help in the Rental Increase Process

- Let your tenant have plenty of notice of their rental increase. The number of days' notice will depend on your type of lease.
- Be ready to deal with tenants who will want to negotiate the rental increases. Be firm and stick to the steps and procedures in your operations manual.
- In my experience, I have found it useful to raise the rent after a lease term, even if it is only a few dollars. This gets the tenant accustomed to the rent being increased at the end of each lease term. Otherwise, a sudden increase after a long positive relationship may cause problems.
- Always be prepared to explain and justify a rent increase. Increases are justifiably made to maintain the property, keep up with the local rental market, and provide new amenities.

Understanding the Timing of a Rental Increase

Telltale signs of when you should raise the rent are:

- When the property's occupancy rate is at 95 percent or higher.
- When you perform a market survey and notice that your rents are priced considerably lower than the local market

CRIME PREVENTION

Using the SEOTA information, you will create an analysis of vulnerability for the property.

- Inspect the premises regularly (inspect what you expect).
- Educate tenants on crime prevention strategies. Give them the proper tools and resources to easily and safely report crimes to proper authorities.
- Use incentives to keep communication lines open. If people are incentivized, they are more likely to get involved.
- Develop relationship with local law enforcement.
- Always quickly respond to tenants' suggestions and complaints about security.
- Maintain and exceed safety requirements:
  - Deadbolts
  - Six-inch screws for doorjambs and locks
  - Interior and exterior lighting
  - Window locks
  - Hedges cut below the windows
  - Signage for security
  - Security systems
  - Dummy cameras to deter criminals
  - Security cage for AC condenser

Safety Techniques

- Always try to deposit money promptly.
- Create and implement systems for safety and review these systems as often as possible.
- Do not allow the door to be closed at the entrance while showing a rental unit to a prospective tenant.

- Do not allow a prospective tenant to get between you and the door, where they could block your line of exit.
- Try to bring someone along when showing a rental unit to a prospective tenant.
- Invest in an alarm device such as a whistle or small siren. (Many car key chain locks come with a panic button that will work well.)
- Work on empty make-ready rental units in the company of at least one other person.
- Have a system for storing residents' door keys. (Typically, keys are stored in a locked cabinet and are coded for an easy-to-use system. The coding system should not indicate building numbers or addresses for the safety of the tenants.)

RISK MANAGEMENT

The most effective way to protect yourself against potential risks to your investment is to create and implement a risk management system.

Here are the building blocks to a successful risk management system:

- Set up policies and procedures to assist in following the risk-management systems.
- Identify any and all potential risks in your operations.
- Create a financial plan to help cover any risks that cannot be assumed or eliminated.
- Create and implement ongoing education, preventive measures, and safety programs.
- Scrutinize the frequency and severity of past potential losses.

You want to make sure these items are addressed:

- Tenant and employee safety
- Liability
- Insurance
- Emergency plan of action

Safety

In the cornerstone of any effective risk-management system, the owner and/or agent should have a strong grasp of policies and procedures and follow those procedures to ensure consistent, safe results.

Author Note: Case Study

I was tasked with stabilizing a forty-unit apartment building. Out of forty units, thirty were occupied. Fifteen were paying rent. Two actually were paying rent on time. The vast majority of those occupants were drug dealers or prostitutes. My job was to stabilize this property. The first step was to remove all of the disruptive occupants, creating an environment that allowed for stabilization using the techniques above. Once these techniques were employed, this made way for the property to begin its stabilization process, which led to the value of the property increasing dramatically.

ORGANIZING YOUR FILES

Staying organized by using technology means efficient time management, reducing errors and cost savings. You have the ability to walk around with a file cabinet in your pocket. You can be instantly prepared, knowledgeable, and qualified for whatever you come across in or out of the office.

You will want to keep everything in a cloud-based storage system. It is also important to have a digital backup of your files and keep hard copies of key documents.

Staying organized is important for many reasons. Most important, doing so will:

- Allow you to be efficient
- Ensure accuracy
- Provide needed documentation:
    - If you are investigated for Fair Housing Law violations
    - If you have to file for eviction
    - If you are sued
    - If you are audited

TIP: Property-Management Hack

While you are developing your business plan (specifically the operational section), you will quickly realize the importance of property management software when managing multiple properties for multiple owners. Depending on your finances, it may be necessary for you to use your own file and organization structure when starting your company. If doing so, we suggest you organize your files using one of these free apps:

- Box or Dropbox
- SignEasy

- Zillow
- Adobe Reader
- CamScanner
- Google Photos

Prospective Tenant File

Keep these in your file for a prospective tenant:

- Rental application
- Guest card
- Copy of driver's license and credit report
- Statement of qualifying criteria move-in cost sheet
- Copies of checks received
- Tenant rejection letter (if denied)
- Pay stubs

Current Tenant File

All of above, plus:

- Lease addendum(s)
- Move-in checklist, rules and regulations form
- Move-in/move-out inspection report
- Copies of all work orders during occupancy
- Copies of all receipts for repairs during occupancy
- Notes and copies of all correspondence with tenant

Corporate File

- Incorporation documents (EINs)
- Insurance documents
- Tax documents
- Template files

Note: Do not delete old files; archive them if necessary. This is important for your legal and tax protection.

THE EVICTION PROCESS

The eviction process is complicated and state specific. I strongly recommend you find a good eviction attorney to work with and build a relationship with them so you know how to work well with each other.

The eviction process is one that must be followed precisely to ensure the rules work in your favor. All the attention you have paid to detail by completing all forms will now pay off for you.

Step 1: Make a copy of the lease agreement, the application, and the late rent notice or other notice you issued. Double-check that the names on the notice match the names on the lease. This is very important.

Step 2: Send the copies to your eviction attorney. Make a call to the attorney after sending the information. They will explain the process to you.

TIPS: During the Eviction Process

1. Remember *not* to accept any rent or monies from the tenant under eviction.
2. If the tenant calls you to ask about the eviction, respond by telling the tenant to please refer any questions to your attorney. This will protect you.
3. If you are evicting a tenant for breaking the rules, remember to document everything! This includes any conversations or actions taken by this tenant.
4. Remember, do not change the language of any notice. If you have any questions, I recommend contacting an eviction attorney.

PROPERTY MANAGEMENT BUSINESS FORMS LIBRARY

The following forms are intended for the property management business operations, meaning these forms are primarily used for interaction between your property management business and your client (owner of the investment property). For more guidance on the use of these forms as well as a *free* editable format of the documents, please visit our website at www.landlordacademy.com.

JOB SPECIFICATION CHECKLIST

(to be submitted to a vendor before work begins)

Date _____

Vendor Name: _____

Insurance: _____

Location of Work to Be Done: _____

Detailed Description of Work to Be Done: _____

_____

_____

Specific Material and Equipment to Be Used: _____

_____

Will Material Be Provided by Vendor?   YES   NO

Additional Material or Equipment Cost: _____

_____

Beginning Date: _____ Completion Date: _____

Time Line of Major Phases of Project: _____

_____

Licenses or Permits Needed: _____

_____

Who is Responsible for Acquiring These? _____

Additional Cost Associated: _____

Included in Total Cost Above or Additional: _____

Clean-Up Required: _____

Additional Cost of Clean-Up: _____

Total Cost (including material, equipment, licenses, permits, clean-up, and any other cost): _____

_____

Payment Schedule: _____

OSHA Requirements: _____

_____

Please provide three or more references.

_____

_____

_____

Management

PROPERTY INTAKE FORM

Owner Name	
Property Address	
Date Management Services Begin	
Existing Tenant	YES NO
Monthly Rental Rate	
Security Deposit Amount	
Last Month's Rent Required	YES NO
Application Fee	
Qualifying Criteria	
Approved with Last Month's Rent	
Pets Allowed (Indicate any Restriction)	YES NO Restriction:
Normal Evictions/No Approval Required	❏ Nonpayment of rent ❏ Illegal Activity ❏ Drug Activity ❏ Other:
Security Deposit Held By	Management Company Owner If owner, list bank account name, address, and number for lease purposes
Owner Authorization for Lease Renewal/Nonrenewal Required?	YES NO
Secondary Contact Person for Owner:	Name: Number:
Repairs Less than or Equal to $250 May Be Handled Without Authorization	YES NO
Security Deposit Deductions Must Be Authorized by Owner	YES NO
Agreed to Minimal Punch List (Requires No Authorization)	❏ Interior Wall Paint ❏ Carpet Cleaning ❏ Cleaning ❏ Locks Changed ❏ A/C Filter Changed
SERVICES REQUIRED	
Management Services (10% of gross collected rent)	YES NO
Marketing/Leasing Services (half of first full month's rent	YES NO
Preventive Maintenance Program	YES NO
Suggested Marketing Actions	Cost—please remit payment
Place for Rent Sign in Yard	Included, no additional charge
List on Website	Included, no additional charge
Share with Network of Alliances	Included, no additional charge

Ad in Newspaper	$
Online Ad	$
Other	

_____   _____
OWNER SIGNATURE   DATE

_____   _____
OWNER SIGNATURE   DATE

_____   _____
MANAGEMENT SIGNATURE   DATE

TENANT NOTICE OF TERMINATION OF MANAGEMENT SERVICES

Date

Tenant
Rental Unit Address
City, State, Zip

Re: Management Services

Dear Tenant:

Please be advised that we will cease to provide management services for the rental property you reside in sixty days from the date of this letter. It has been a pleasure working with you.

You should receive notification from the owner of your rental property, or a management company on their behalf, instructing you where to make rent payments and to submit maintenance requests. We will be unable to accept any funds or accommodate any requests sixty days after this notice.

You will also by law receive notification of where your security deposit will be transferred and held on your behalf.

Sincerely,

NOTICE OF TERMINATION OF MANAGEMENT SERVICES

Date

Owner
Address
City, State, Zip

Re: Management of (Rental Unit Address)

Dear (Owner Name):

Please consider this correspondence as my sixty-day written notice of cancellation of my management services for the above-referenced property(ies). Our services will cease sixty days after the date of this notice. Please be advised that we are forced to cease managing your property(ies) due to the following:

[LIST REASONS]

Please be advised we will be sending a letter to all tenants advising them of this change within the next two weeks.

We are currently holding rental funds and escrow funds as itemized on the attached reports. We will maintain the escrow funds for up to thirty days after the date our services cease for availability of pending expenses on your behalf. All remaining funds will be transferred to you in no more than thirty days after the date our services cease.

According to Florida law, we may transfer any security deposit or advance rents to a licensed real estate broker, or if permission is granted in writing by the tenant, we may transfer these funds into a separate Florida bank account that you have set up. Please contact us with instructions pertaining to the transfer of security deposits.

Note: You may continue to be liable to our firm for management fees/commissions, as we have been forced to take this action due to circumstances beyond our control.

Sincerely,

THIS FORM IS A STARTING POINT AND LEGAL ADVICE IS RECOMMENDED BEFORE USE. Security deposits have many legalities that impact their transfer.

NOTICE OF EVICTION PROCEEDING

Date

Owner
Address
City, State, Zip

Re: Notice of Eviction Proceeding for (Rental Property Address)

Dear Owner:
Please be advised that I have initiated eviction proceedings for the above-referenced property for the following reason(s):
    [LIST REASONS]
    Pursuant to our Management Agreement, prior authorization is not necessary for this action.
    The cost of an eviction of this manner will be approximately _____.
    COST
    _____ This cost will be deducted from your Escrow funds.
    _____ Please write a check for the above amount.

Sincerely,

NOTICE OF VENDOR SERVICES

Date

Owner
Address
City, State, Zip

Re: Vendor Services for (Rental Property Address)

Dear Owner:
Please be advised that I have utilized the services of the following Vendor for the following reason on your behalf:
    Vendor Name:
    Reason:
    Cost:
    COST
    _____ The cost indicated above will be deducted from your Escrow funds.
    _____ Please remit funds in the amount of _____ to cover this cost.
    AUTHORIZATION
    _____ According to our Management Agreement, permission is not necessary for this action.
    _____ Please initial here to authorize this action on your behalf.

Sincerely,

NOTICE OF MAINTENANCE ISSUE COMPLETED

Date

Owner
Address
City, State, Zip

Re: Notice of Maintenance Issue Completed for (Rental Property Address)

Dear Owner:
Please be advised that the maintenance issue below has been successfully completed.
    Type of Service: _____
    Vendor Name: _____
    _____ In response to tenant complaint
    _____ Other:
    Cost: _____
    No further action is needed.

Thank you,

LEASING REQUEST FORM

Please e-mail to [e-mail address] within five business days so I can handle this issue effectively on your behalf.

Date

Owner
Address
City, State, Zip

Re: Leasing Request Form for (Rental Property Address)

Dear Owner:
Please be advised that the above-referenced property is scheduled to be available for release on _____.
    Reason:
    _____ Nonrenewal of Lease at Owner/Management Discretion
    _____ Nonrenewal of Lease at Tenant's Discretion
    _____ Termination of Lease at Tenant's Discretion
    _____ Eviction Proceeding Under Way
    _____ Other
    Please instruct me if you would like our company to handle the marketing and/or leasing of this property. Please note that hard costs involved in marketing will be your responsibility. Our Leasing Service fee equal to half the first full month's total will be applied.

Sincerely,

OWNER RESPONSE

_____ Please proceed with marketing.
_____ Please proceed with leasing services.
_____ Please call me to discuss further.

Date: _____

REQUEST FOR MAINTENANCE APPROVAL

E-mail to [e-mail address] within two business days.

Date

Owner
Address
City, State, Zip

Re: Request for Maintenance Approval for (Rental Property Address)

Dear Owner:
I am requesting approval for the following maintenance service for the above-referenced property as follows:
　　Type of Service: _____
　　Vendor Name: _____
　　____ In response to tenant complaint
　　____ Other:
　　Cost: _____
COST
　　_____ The cost indicated above will be deducted from your Escrow funds.
　　_____ Please remit funds in the amount of _____ to cover this cost.

Sincerely,

OWNER RESPONSE

_____ I authorize the above maintenance action.
_____ I do not authorize the above maintenance action.
_____ Please call me to discuss further.

Date: _____

NOTICE OF COMPLIANCE

NO RESPONSE NECESSARY

Date:

Owner
Address
City, State, Zip

Re: Notice of Compliance for (Rental Property Address)

Dear Owner:
Please be advised that the above-referenced tenant has complied with the notice (enclosed). No further action is required at this time.

Sincerely,

NOTICE OF MAINTENANCE ACTION

Date

Owner
Address
City, State, Zip

Re: Maintenance Action for (Rental Property Address)

Dear Owner:
Please be advised that I have coordinated maintenance services for the above-referenced property as follows:
Type of Service: _____
Vendor Name: _____
_____ In response to tenant complaint
_____ Other:
Cost: _____
COST
_____ The cost indicated above will be deducted from your Escrow funds.
_____ Please remit funds in the amount of _____ to cover this cost.
AUTHORIZATION
_____ According to our Management Agreement, permission is not necessary for this action.

Sincerely,

RECOMMENDATION OF LEASE RENEWAL OR NONRENEWAL

E-mail to [e-mail address] within five business days so I can handle this issue effectively on your behalf.

Date

Owner
Address
City, State, Zip

Re: Recommendation of Lease Renewal or Nonrenewal for (Rental Property Address)

Dear Owner:
Please be advised the lease term for the above-referenced property will end in ninety days. I recommend the lease be:

_____ Renewed

_____ Nonrenewed

Reason: [If any] _____

After conducting a market survey to compare current rental rates, I recommend the rent for the above-referenced property be increased to _____.

Sincerely,

OWNER RESPONSE

_____ I agree with your lease renewal or nonrenewal recommendation above.

_____ I agree with your suggested rental rate increase above.

_____ Please call me to discuss further.

Date: _____

REQUEST FOR ESCROW REPLENISHMENT

Date

Owner
Address
City, State, Zip

Re: Request for Escrow Replenishment for (Rental Property Address)

Dear Owner:
Please be advised that the escrow funds for the above-referenced property are: _____.

Per our Management Agreement, this amount should be no less than $250.00.

Please remit additional funds in the amount of _____ as soon as possible to allow our company to handle the needs of your investment property efficiently on your behalf.

Thank you,

EVICTION RECOMMENDATION FORM

E-mail to [e-mail address] within two business days so I can handle this issue effectively on your behalf.

Date

Owner
Address
City, State, Zip

Re: Eviction Recommendation Form for (Rental Property Address)

Dear Owner:
Please be advised that I am recommending initiating an eviction proceeding for the above-referenced property for the following reason:

The cost of an eviction in this manner will be approximately _____.

COST

_____ Check here to have the cost indicated above deducted from your Escrow funds.

_____ Check here if you plan to remit costs to me in the amount above.

Sincerely,

OWNER RESPONSE

_____ Please proceed with the eviction.
_____ Do not proceed with the eviction.
_____ Please call me to discuss further.
Date: _____

RECOMMENDATION FOR ISSUANCE OF NOTICE

E-mail to [e-mail address] within two business days so I can handle this issue effectively on your behalf.

Date

Owner
Address
City, State, Zip

Re: Recommendation for Issuance of Notice for (Rental Property Address)

Dear Owner:
Please be advised that I am recommending issuance of the following notice for the following reason:
   Notice:
   Reason:

Sincerely,

OWNER RESPONSE

_____ Please proceed with issuing notice.
_____ Do not proceed with issuing notice.
_____ Please call me to discuss further.

Date: _____

INTRODUCTION OF NEW MANAGEMENT TO TENANT

Date

Owner
Address
City, State, Zip

Re: Management Services

Dear Tenant:
We are excited to announce that our company will begin handling the management of your residents on _____. Providing quality housing and great service is important to our company. We look forward to helping provide you with a wonderful place to call home.

Beginning with the rent for the month of _____ please send rent payments to the following address: _____.

We are also requesting that you sign the new enclosed lease. This lease provides you with important information, including where your security deposit is now being held and how to contact us with maintenance and repair needs. The lease does not increase your rent, nor does it extend the length of your original lease term. It simply updates relevant matters now that we will be assisting you with your housing needs.

We are also enclosing photos of our team so you can recognize us next time we meet.

Please sign the attached lease and return in the enclosed envelope at your earliest convenience.

We look forward to working with you.

Sincerely,

RESPONSE TO OWNER SECURITY DEPOSIT REQUEST

Date

Owner
Address
City, State, Zip

Re: Your Security Deposit Request for (Rental Property Address)

Dear Owner:
This correspondence is in response to your request for deductions from the security deposit for the above-referenced address.

It is the opinion of our legal counsel that these/this amount(s) (are only wear and tear, are not legally deductible, should not be deducted, etc.)

By deducting these amounts you will expose yourself to a potential lawsuit by the tenant. In the event the tenant is able to prove you were not legally permitted to make the deduction, you may be held liable for the disputed amount, your attorney's fees, and those of the tenant plus any costs of suit.

We will make the deductions per your request unless we are immediately notified to do otherwise by you in writing. Time is of the essence as we have only a fifteen-day time period from the date that the tenant vacated.

Your success as an investor is important to us and we feel this decision may cause you to incur liability as well as appear unprofessional to your tenant.

We encourage you to reconsider.

Sincerely,

VENDOR DETAIL CHECKLIST

Legal Company Name _____

d/b/a _____

Contact/Representative _____

Address _____

Phone _____ Cell _____

E-mail _____

Federal Tax ID Number _____

Business License Number(s) _____

Type of Entity: Corp _____ LLC _____ Partnership _____ Sole Prop _____

Liability Ins. Carrier _____

Policy Number(s) _____

Workers Compensation _____

Policy Numbers _____

Executed This _____ Day of _____ 20____

I certify that the above is true and correct and that I am an authorized company representative. I agree that I will not hold the property management company, its agents, employees, or assigns liable for the payment for any work performed or materials provided for the properties which are or were managed by the property management company.

Vendor Signature

RESPONSE TO OWNER REPAIR REFUSAL

Date

Owner
Address
City, State, Zip

Re: Your Refusal for Repairs for (Rental Property Address)

Dear Owner:
This correspondence is in response to your refusal to authorize the following repairs for the above-referenced address:

It is our professional opinion and the opinion of our legal counsel that these items are your responsibility and should be repaired/replaced immediately at your expense.

We will take no further action regarding this repair/replacement until further written notice from you and upon receipt of sufficient funds to cover such repair/replacement. Our company will not be held liable for any litigation that may arise out of the failure to make the repair/replacement.

Please note that your tenant may withhold rent, call code enforcement or other governmental authorities, possibly attempt a repair themselves, break the lease, and/or hold you liable for damages or sue you if the repair/replacement is not made. In the event of a lawsuit, Florida law provides that the prevailing party may recover all attorney's fees and costs, thus you will have to pay both your attorney and the tenant's attorney.

Your success as an investor is important to us and we feel this decision may cause you to incur liability as well as appear unprofessional to your tenant.

We encourage you to reconsider.

Sincerely,

NOTICE OF FUNDS DUE

Date

Owner
Address
City, State, Zip

Re: Funds Due for (Rental Property Address)

Dear Owner:
Please be advised that you owe funds to our company in the total amount of _____.
    Itemization:
    Expense:
    Amount:
    _____ funds in the amount of _____ will be deducted from your remaining funds in Escrow for rental property located at _____.
    _____ Please remit the amount indicated above upon receipt of this notice.

Sincerely,

RECEIPT FOR FUNDS COLLECTED

NO RESPONSE NECESSARY

Date

Owner
Address
City, State, Zip

Amount Received:
For Rental Property Address:
Placed in:
_____ Escrow Account
_____ Operating Account
_____ Security Deposit Account

_____
Property Manager
Date: _____

OWNER DISBURSEMENT METHOD

Date

Owner
Address
City, State, Zip

Re: Disbursement of Owner Funds

_____ Please mail my disbursements to me:
Check payable to:
Mailing Address:
_____ Please electronically transfer my disbursements:
Name on Bank Account:
Bank:
Routing Number:
Account Number:
My SSN or EIN is: _____

_____
Owner Signature
Date: _____

INTRODUCTION OF NEW MANAGEMENT TO TENANT

Date

Tenant
Rental Unit Address
City, State, Zip

Re: Management Services

Dear Tenant:
We are excited to announce that our company will begin handling the management of your residents on _____. Providing quality housing and great service is important to our company. We look forward to helping provide you with a wonderful place to call home.

Beginning with the rent for the month of _____ please send rent payments to the following address: _____.

We are also requesting you sign the new enclosed lease. This lease provides you with important information, including where your security deposit is now being held and how to contact us with maintenance and repair needs. The lease does not increase your rent, nor does it extend the length of your original lease term. It simply updates relevant matters now that we will be assisting you with your housing needs.

We are also enclosing photos of our team so you can recognize us next time we meet.

Please sign the attached lease and return in the enclosed envelope at your earliest convenience.

We look forward to working with you.

Sincerely,

NOTICE OF TERMINATION DUE TO SALE OF PREMISES

TO: _____   DATE _____

_____

_____

YOU ARE HEREBY ADVISED THAT YOUR TENANCY AND/OR LEASE IF APPLICABLE WILL BE TERMI-NATED EARLY DUE TO THE SALE OF OR CONTRACT FOR SALE OF THE PREMISES IN WHICH YOU RESIDE. YOU MUST VACATE THE PREMISES NO LATER THAN _____, 20_____. THIS ACTION IS TAKEN IN ACCORDANCE WITH THE TERMS OF YOUR LEASE AGREEMENT. NO EXTENSIONS SHALL BE GRANTED VERBALLY, AND IF ANY EXTENSIONS ARE GRANTED, THE EXTENSION MUST BE IN WRITING AND SIGNED BY ALL PAR-TIES. IN THE EVENT THAT YOU DO NOT VACATE THE PREMISES BY SAID DATE, LEGAL ACTION MAY BE TAKEN.

_____

Owner/Agent Signature and Printed Name

_____

Property/Company Name

_____

Property/Company Address

_____

Telephone Number

CERTIFICATE OF SERVICE

I hereby certify that a copy of the above notice was:

_____ delivered to _____ by hand

_____ posted on the premises described above in the tenant's absence

on _____, 20_____.

By:_____

   Owner/Agent

SIX

THE NO-FAIL APPROACH TO LANDING CLIENTS

The fundamental systems and services that will help you attract and keep clients

If you've gotten this far, you've probably seen that property management is not a get-rich-quick scheme. You don't have to be a rocket scientist to be successful, but you can't just roll over one morning and sign a contract to manage millions of dollars' worth of property, either. You will need to put in the time to learn the ropes and gather experience. But as you do this, you'll be much more attractive to potential clients. Why? Because multimillionaire investors don't have the time to manage their properties, nor do they have time to effectively learn how to manage their properties. They are more than willing to delegate this task, but they will only delegate to someone whom they know and trust to be highly skilled and competent. And these days, you can't just *say* that you're highly skilled and competent—you have to prove it. The best way to market your property management company is to become a recognized expert in the field of property management.

Let me let you in on a little secret: Publishing my first book, *Buy It, Rent It, Profit!*, in 2009 didn't guarantee my success in the real estate industry. Sure, I had some experience under my belt, but I lost a lot in the housing crash and had to rebuild just like everyone else. People would always say that all you had to do to build your business was to publish a book, and while I am grateful for the opportunity to reach so many people through *Buy It, Rent It, Profit!* and *The Landlord Entrepreneur*, my real estate business has only continued to grow because of the work I've done to build my personal brand, by traveling around my home state of Florida to speak to different housing associations and building an online presence. And it was through that brand building that I was able to secure contracts with some of the largest housing associations in the country, develop partnerships with some of the greatest providers of real estate industry resources, and sign on to coach countless individuals who want to establish their own property management companies.

And as I advise many of my coaching clients, there is a simple, three-step process to building a brand that attracts more business than you can handle.

Step 1: Get Educated. This book is a great start, but I encourage you to visit landlord academy.com and view our numerous free resources to get an even greater understanding of the real estate industry and property management.

Step 2: Teach. The best way to verify that you really have expert-level knowledge on the subject of property management is to start booking speaking gigs for yourself. You probably won't make any money starting out, but you'll have a captive audience of people who want to hear what you have to say. And if you can hold their attention and answer their questions, that's a good sign.

Try contacting your local housing associations or real estate brokerages to ask if you can offer a free seminar to their members or employees. Just remember to treat it like a well-paid gig, even though you're likely not getting paid at all. In addition to providing the necessary training you need to hone your message, these speaking engagements will also develop you as a go-to resource in your local community. When people think "property management" they will eventually start to think of you, and investors will begin to seek out your services.

Step 3: Go Online. The third part of your marketing process is to develop a web presence that will firmly establish you as an authority in the real estate industry. I personally tried to avoid doing this for years, but eventually I came to the realization that in today's society, if you are not branding yourself, you are quickly becoming obsolete.

The good news is that this method of branding yourself doesn't require a lot of money. I didn't spend money on commercials, advertising, banners, direct mail, or anything like that. I spent money on training and educating myself, and then going out and educating individuals for free, conducting free seminars and workshops for whoever would listen.

If you do want to spend money, I would tell you to spend it on a good web designer. You need someone who can make you look as professional as possible online because, at the end of the day, people will go to your website and form their impressions about you from their very first visit. And as you speak at more and more events and begin to become recognized as a thought leader, people are going to Google you and see what you're doing online. It's the twenty-first century, and that's just the way it is. And I can guarantee you that if you don't have a professional presence online, your chances of developing a successful property management business will be severely limited.

Now, let's look at some strategies to develop a high-quality and highly trafficked website.

CREATE GREAT CONTENT

When my web developer, Nathan Johnson, first told me that a website is a living thing, I didn't believe him. I actually thought he was crazy. But he's not. He's absolutely right. Establishing a blog on your site gives you the opportunity to connect directly with readers, some of whom will later become your clients. You can share your knowledge with them and they will then share it with others. The key to instigating that process is to create content that people actually want to consume.

Before we post any blog posts or videos online, my team and I do a lot of research first. Sure, I'm considered a real estate expert, and it would be easy for me to sit down and come up with a couple of dozen article topics that I think people are interested in. But what if I'm wrong? What if, instead of learning about how to hire an in-house maintenance staff for their property management company, readers actually want tips on how to contract with a reputable third-party maintenance company? Gaining this insider knowledge before you create content ensures not only that you won't waste time writing blogs or recording videos that no one cares about, but also that people will be more likely to find you through organic searches when they search for the exact topics you're writing or speaking about.

So how can you start to conduct this research? Find real estate forums online, like the one at landlordacademy.com, and read what people are talking about and see what questions they're asking. Quora.com is also a great tool for getting into the minds of your target customers/clients. You should also visit the sites of other property management companies to see what they're talking about; eventually, you'll start to see some trends. This is also your opportunity to join some other conversations because the reality is that just building a website won't make people visit it. You need to get out and start making a name for yourself online so that people can start to get to know you and put a name and face to your message.

When it comes to social media, I recommend only creating accounts on channels that you know you can stay consistent with. The idea is to go deep, not wide, so if you can only focus your efforts on one platform at a time, start there. Then build as many relationships as you can and share as much free content as you can before moving on to another platform.

One more tip on creating online content: If you're trying to decide between written and video content, I would suggest videos. With video, people are going to be able to watch, engage, and learn. Then, from the video, you can take the exact same content and transcribe it into a blog, to create something for visitors to your site who would rather read their content. And then you can put that on your website. You can also create snippets of the video to share on Facebook, as well as posting it in its entirety on YouTube. So when you create video, you are getting so much mileage out of the same piece of content, and in the process you're gaining more traction, more engagement, and more business opportunities.

This is just a brief overview of what's really possible online, and there are much more thorough resources that I highly recommend, including *Jab, Jab, Jab, Right Hook: How to Tell Your Story in a Noisy Social World,* by Gary Vaynerchuk; *Launch: An Internet Millionaire's Secret Formula to Sell Almost Anything Online, Build a Business You Love, and Live the Life of Your Dreams,* by Jeff Walker; and *Platform: Get Noticed in a Noisy World*, by Michael Hyatt.

The most important point I want you to take away is this: These techniques work. They have literally changed my entire business. I'm not just telling you things that I've heard; I'm telling you things that I know because I literally had to rebuild everything after recovering from a brain tumor that almost killed me—and that was after publishing a bestselling book with one of the biggest and most prestigious publishers in the world. Like many other people, I thought, "A website is just a website." But it's not. A website has the capability to revolutionize your company and take your business to levels you never imagined.

Once you understand how to establish yourself as a thought leader in the world of property management and begin to build your brand, you will find it much easier to attract quality client prospects as you naturally discuss your business and services. The question then becomes: "How do I convert these prospects into signed clients?"

And that, friend, may actually be the easiest part of the process.

UNDERSTANDING YOUR CLIENTS AND THEIR GOALS

In order to attract and convert leads, you need to thoroughly understand your clients and their goals.

There are many types of owners and important characteristics and mind-sets they operate under. The reason for investment is key to understanding your owners. As a property manager, whether you are a beginner or experienced, you will quickly understand you are going to meet various property owners and properties. There are going to be different categories that these owners can be placed in. The terms in the management agreement need to reflect these variables.

- Capital appreciation—similar to a retirement fund. This is a long-term growth strategy. This type of investor is typically looking for less risk. This investor typically will not need an immediate return on investment and is able to reinvest cash flows back into the property, strengthening their position for long-term appreciation.
- Cash flow—similar to the day trader. These investors have a focus on a positive income stream and immediate returns. Economies of scale will play a big role to offset risk, that is, protect cash flow. The interview process is very important for this type of owner. If this investor needs immediate income to pay their personal bills and does not have the benefits of economies of scale, there will be a lot of pressure on the management to provide perfect cash flow results that likely are not realistic. There are many variables out of the control of the property manager.
- Distressed income properties—poor asset selection, poor management, poor financing leads to an asset not performing to the desired cash flow. In our experience we have come across a lot of properties that people purchased from a wholesaler that was a great deal for the wholesaler but not for the investor. The investor then finds out that there are unforeseen barriers to a positive NOI. In these cases, they have

likely overpaid and have few resources left. This type of owner will be particularly challenging. They are going to require a lot of your time, and time is money that they might not have. You may need to be creative with the management agreement terms to arrive at a realistic win-win.

We are not saying that anything is good or bad; these are considerations to make. There are opportunities in distressed properties and challenging market conditions. What we are saying is, be realistic about what it will take to achieve the goals of the owner, the property, and the property management. Make sure these goals align before you take on the project.

BUILDING YOUR BRAND THROUGH SOCIAL MEDIA

Consider the items below to make sure that your website is effectively helping you to promote your brand and your goals. Remember, your most important employee, even if you're a single operator, is your website: it's constantly working for you 24/7.

- **Content/blogs:** Remember: In order to skyrocket to the top of the SEO charts, you must provide valuable content that people are searching for.
- **Lead nurturing:** To gather leads from your site, know what to say and how to say it. Once you have a lead, know how to develop a relationship with your prospective client.
- **Reputation:** All the social media and marketing will not stack up to a hill of beans if the individual brand has no credibility in the marketplace.
- **Pay-per-lead:** Note that 80 percent of searches are done by tenants, 10 percent by prospective clients. KNOW YOUR INDUSTRY TO ATTRACT THE PROSPECTS.
- **Pay-per-click:** This tool is used by companies attempting to brand themselves by paying for visits to their site by the visitor finding them through an ad rather than an organic search. If you decide to use PPC, make sure your website is providing useful content for your prospective client.
- **Teaching/training:** Clients nowadays are tired of being sold—they want to be educated. Educational content is the best way to communicate to clients why your services provide the answer to their problems.
- **Technology:** Successful branding weighs heavily on your website. Gone are the days of having to be a programmer: the most widely used website platform is WordPress, which I have personally found to be extremely user-friendly. You can create your own website using the WordPress platform, but I also recommend outsourcing such work to a capable web designer who can help you create and grow your brand. You can also expand your branding ecosystem by using Facebook, Instagram, Twitter, LinkedIn, and other social media, blogs, and email lists.
- **Growth plan:** Client acquisition expense (per rental property) = expense of marketing (div) # of rental properties acquired.

For example, if your marketing expense is $250 per rental property and you want to grow the number of rental units by one hundred properties, your marketing budget is $25,000 a year. Divide that by twelve and you will establish your monthly marketing budget.

EFFECTIVE COMMUNICATION

Communication is vital for property management success from generating leads and converting them to maintaining them. You need to be able to accurately get your message across to show your ability to provide results to the owner. Various types of communication will be determined by several owner factors. Strive to provide easy accessibility and documentation.

- Types of owners (Do you need screening or direct access?)
- Location of the owner (Time zone difference)
- Communication preferences (Phone, text, e-mail, online portal, mail)
- Scope of work (Is a video of progress desired or simply confirmation of completion?)

Property Management Hacks

We have found that Ruby Receptionists provides great value and delivers ideal solutions for our management communication. They ensure incoming calls are reliably and professionally answered and that immediate information is provided to caller and management.

Understand that each client is different. Create a custom management strategy for each client that will facilitate meeting both client and management goals.

Understand the effects of being proactive versus reactive, specifically with respect to time for the management company.

FIRST CONTACT—LEAD GENERATION

Regardless of how you are generating leads, be it from teaching a class or an unexpected introduction, always be prepared. Have your elevator pitch ready. Collect their contact information and get the lead into your CRM (customer relation management) to develop. Follow through with setting the second key appointment.

SECOND CONTACT—OWNER INTERVIEW

This is the most critical and most often overlooked process. Using the effective communication method, strive for a face-to-face meeting. This is when you will gather the information necessary to prepare you for the proposal. Understand your client and their goals. This is an opportunity for you to insert yourself as an industry leader by being able to anticipate their needs in advance, provide systems, and create a proposal.

- Goals
- Strategies
- Financing
- Property criteria
- Ownership
- Exit strategy

THIRD CONTACT—CLOSE

This is where you are going to give a detailed plan of action on how you will achieve the goals of the owner. Give an explanation of your strategic recommendations and show how your success is tied to theirs.

Now that we have taken you through the three stages of lead conversion, I am providing you with a sample management proposal. Your property management company's success depends on your ability to develop a customizable management proposal. On the following pages, you will find a detailed proposal template that you can submit to any client prospect. Instead of just telling you what to do and what to say to secure the contract, I thought it would be most informative to *show* you. Reading through this proposal will help you to further understand what is expected of your company if you plan to operate at the highest level, and, most important, it will show your prospects that they can entrust you with their valuable investments.

MANAGEMENT PROPOSAL

Your Property Management Company's Name Here _____
Your Mission Statement Here _____
Now that you understand your client's goals, you are ready to create a customized proposal for your client. Typical management proposals should include the following:

- Define purpose—your company's vision
- Services to be provided—demonstrate consistency
- Who will provide services—define what you are responsible for and display vendor relations
- How services will be performed—details of how each requirement will be completed
- Fee structure—spells out how much the services will cost

THE LANDLORD
PROPERTY MANAGEMENT
ACADEMY®

PROPERTY OWNER'S HANDBOOK

INTRODUCTION

Use this section to define your company's unique sales proposition; take the time to really distinguish your business brand and its services. This section should be well thought out, and your website should reflect much of what is listed in this section. Remember, there are a lot of so-called thought leaders out there with new blogs; this is your opportunity to show your prospective client why building a relationship with you and your business will be a rewarding and profitable experience.

Our purpose for the Property Owner's Handbook is to first help you, the property owner, to better understand the administrative and management systems of (**Your Property Management Company**). Second, it is to help provide valuable industry knowledge and insight. It is our pleasure to introduce you to our company and to answer any questions that involve our company or the industry as a whole. When property owners are provided with industry knowledge and tools, we have found it provides them with a greater understanding of the day-to-day operations of property management. This then enables those owners to hold a property management company accountable for its performance, putting both parties on the same page and allowing for a better working relationship.

We achieve this in our company by providing each owner with a scholarship to attend a training course at The Landlord Property Management Academy™. The Academy was founded by Bryan Chavis, author of the industry bestseller *Buy It, Rent It, Profit!*, and is nationally recognized for providing the highest-quality rental investor, landlord, and property management courses. Our team obtained their training and education through the Academy, and we believe it is a great resource to help you better understand the field of property management and the services we will provide you. The Academy is also a great source for providing up-to-date industry news and information. For more on The Landlord Property Management Academy, including online courses, please visit landlordacademy.com.

Author insight: As you can see, we use education to create a relationship with our clients; over the years I have found that this approach works best to break the ice and allow our property management company to highlight our skills, thereby building trust between our management company and the client.

Please note: Our business relationship is formed in writing between you, the property owner, and (**Your Property Management Company**), through a document called the management agreement. All procedures, terms, services, and conditions detailed in this proposal are subject to change, withdrawal, or modification at any time and could take place without notice. You should look solely to your individual management agreement for actual services rendered.

Our team in advance thanks you for taking the time to understand our business. We look forward to serving you and your business.

*(**Your Property Management Company**) IS AN EQUAL HOUSING PROVIDER.*

*(**Your Property Management Company**) does business in accordance with the Fair Housing Act and does not discriminate on the basis of race, creed, religion, age, sex, familial status, marital status, disability, color, national origin, sexual orientation, or any other protected classes.*

CONTENTS

(YOUR PROPERTY MANAGEMENT COMPANY) MAKES INVESTING AND OWNING RENTAL PROPERTY EASY

In this section, you are going to distinguish yourself from the competition. Detail your value add and make sure to point out what you can do that others can't, specifically through your training and education. See the sample below. You want to really focus on how interacting with your business will benefit your client in the long term. Remember, there are a lot of so-called thought leaders out there. Let the client know why building a relationship with your business will be beneficial to them.

A big part of success in real estate—and business in general—can be attributed to forming the right types of alliances. Alliances increase strategic positioning and are used as a method to increase strengths, helping all involved parties to reach their goals more efficiently and at a much quicker pace. At (**Your Property Management Company**), we are committed to this philosophy. In fact we built our name on it.

1. **Each member of our team is a certified property manager.**
   One of our team's biggest strengths is that all team members have received their professional property management certification. This intensive training is only available through the nationally recognized Landlord Academy, and in addition to helping our team members to become the most effective property managers in the industry, this designation must be renewed on an annual basis, ensuring that our team members stay abreast of all legal and industry changes. This designation helps ensure that your property will be managed by a very elite group of well-trained property managers.

2. **We employ comprehensive tenant screening and qualification procedures.**
   One of the most powerful ways to reduce late rents, problem tenants, and evictions is through proactive tenant screening. We create custom qualifying criteria through the SEOTA evaluation for each property to maximize NOI. Ineffective qualifying

criteria erode the value of tenant screening. All prospective tenants will be screened using The Landlord Property Management Academy's tenant screening program. The Academy has partnered with TransUnion's SmartMove to provide one of the most comprehensive screening platforms in the nation, effectively evaluating prospects on past evictions, criminal record, rental history, credit history, work history, and other factors. To view a free demo of the tenant screening process, we encourage you to visit our website (insert your website name).

3. **Efficiency through property management software.**

   Full-service property management software is a cost-saving tool for a rental investor/owner. It provides accurate, efficient tracking of rents collected, late rents, vacancies, maintenance costs, and more. While off-the-shelf accounting programs may provide tools like a balance sheet, profit-and-loss statement, aged receivables, and other financial reports, they do not include property-related reports such as rent rolls, vacancy listings, or lease expiration reports. Property management software (refer to the website for suggestions of preferred software) combines modern accounting and property management features to provide our team—and you—with an all-inclusive solution. This enables us to provide you with a wide range of detailed reports that will better enable you to track the performance of your investment.

4. **We provide easy communication.**

   We are available by phone, text, e-mail, postal mail, or personal appointments, and our team is always ready to assist you.

5. **We contract with experienced service personnel.**

   Maintenance, repairs, and other services are always performed by licensed and insured vendors. As part of our team's Professional Property Management™ training, we have specific training that helps us to better monitor the work of vendors and also to implement our preventive maintenance program.

6. **We provide detailed property inspections.**

   We can provide, as a special service, written comprehensive inspection reports, including photos or video of your property during tenancies and after.

7. **We offer free consultations and training.**

   Through our partnership with The Landlord Property Management Academy™, we have arranged to provide you with additional advice about how to evaluate potential rental areas, how to invest in rental properties, how to prepare your property for rent, and how to better understand the current market rents. Also be sure to ask about our Owner Workshop Program. Some of the listed workshops, including Rental Investing 101™ (a comprehensive study of the current market conditions) and Building a Foundation in Property Management™ (an overview of all aspects of property management), provide you with industry knowledge to help better gauge property management services.

8. **We use an owner-friendly management agreement.**
   There are no restrictive clauses, no hidden fees for services, and no difficult termination clauses. Just an easy-to-read and understandable management agreement.

FREQUENTLY ASKED QUESTIONS ABOUT (YOUR PROPERTY MANAGEMENT COMPANY)

This is an opportunity for you to answer a lot of questions you will get from clients. This will demonstrate your knowledge and your ability to anticipate client needs in advance. Below is a list we have comprised from our experience. Showing your prospective clients that you are able to anticipate their real estate investment needs is key to gaining their respect and trust. This will also help to separate you from the competition.

Q: What makes (Your Property Management Company) different from other companies?
A: This is a very common question, and we provide a very easy answer: You can trust that our team is among the most well trained in the business. We also offer our Owner Workshop Program, a very unique training program that provides seminars to all our owners, covering topics such as Rental Investing 101™ (a comprehensive study of the current market conditions) and Building a Foundation in Property Management™ (a comprehensive study of all aspects of property management). These workshops are used as a tool to help you stay up-to-date with any industry changes that may impact your portfolio. These programs also allow you to gain industry knowledge that will help you to better gauge our level of service.

As an investor, you may also take part in our Rental Portfolio Checkup, an analysis designed to specifically evaluate your rental portfolio, then strategically plan out your investment strategy according to the current real estate market conditions. You may also choose to have your investment portfolio analyzed from a legal standpoint. If so, we'd be happy to refer you to one of the leading law firms in the state that specializes in asset protection. This firm will then evaluate and/or create corporate entities that may be used to protect your real estate portfolio.

We're not required to offer these additional services; we choose to do it because we care about you and the success of your investments.

Q: What types of properties does (Your Property Management Company) manage?
A: We primarily focus our services on residential single-family, duplex, and multifamily properties. However, this does not preclude us from providing management for select commercial properties.

Q: What are the office hours of (Your Property Management Company)?
A: We are open for business from 9:00 a.m. to 5:00 p.m. weekdays. After hours and on weekends we always have an emergency contact on call.

Q: How does (Your Property Management Company) handle emergencies?
A: A big part of good landlord-tenant relations is availability and a timely response. Our company provides an on-call person twenty-four hours a day to handle emergencies. We have a preferred list of service vendors who will respond promptly to all emergencies.

Q: How does (Your Property Management Company) perform bookkeeping services and report that information to property owners?
A: With our preferred property management software, we are able to send you detailed property reports at your request:

- Rent roll report—shows the move-in/move-out date, security deposit, tenant finances
- Profit and loss statement—shows the specific property income versus expenses
- Vacancy report—current and future vacancies
- Detailed maintenance report—evaluates reactive versus proactive cost benefit
- Delinquency report—identifies income leaks that negatively impact cash flow (NOI)
- General ledger report—shows all accounts
- Bank reconciliation report—shows all money in and out
- Security account reports, operating account reports—accounts of deposits held

Tip: Inspect what you expect. The only way balance sheets will balance is if you are constantly monitoring the finances through detailed reports. Accounting reports show the economic position of the asset, and the ability to forecast and stay proactive relies on accurate finances.

Creating a financial reporting system is key for every property management business, as well as for the properties themselves. Financial maintenance allows you to be proactive and stay ahead of issues. A small amount of delinquent rent that is just past due is easier to collect than three months past-due rent. Rental property should adhere to this system within your overall operations manual; every team member should understand the system and apply it to each property and the overall business itself. Typically, a property manager and owner will want some of the same reports. Some of the basic reports should be run on a monthly basis; however, some owners may want various types of reports on a weekly basis. A property manager may want to run reports frequently, especially when market trends shift; they may want to look at occupancy levels and vacancy reports to get a handle on the current and upcoming rental climate.

When reporting, there are some fundamentals that typically revolve around what is known as the accounting month-end process. At the end of each month, certain reports are usually generated from the property management company. The property management company is typically using cloud-based software that will allow the business to generate custom reports.

How detailed the reports are and how many are generated depends on the type of rental property; single-family reporting is typically more straightforward than multifamily, retail, and office buildings.

Auditors look for accounting systems to be straightforward and seamless. Auditors are more frequently going to scrutinize your banking accounts, typically known as trust accounts or operating and security deposit accounts. These accounts must be well maintained. Auditors may look to review supporting documents such as the following:

1. Bank statements—you will also want to include canceled checks, deposit slips, and bank receipts; your operations manual will have a detailed system for this process, located in this book's day-to-day operations chapter.
2. Owner statements
3. Receipts and disbursements journals/ledgers with:
   - Total deposits
   - Deposit dates
   - Total amounts
   - Client the funds are held for
   - Account disbursements names, dates, and dollar amounts
4. Client ledgers—these ledgers will need to be available for both the owners and the tenants

Management software will make accessing these detailed reports very easy.

Q: Will (Your Property Management Company) deposit an owner's checks directly into the bank?
A: We will deposit your distribution check directly into your bank, either by mail or electronic deposit, and send the monthly statement to you.

Q: How much does (Your Property Management Company) charge for management services?
A: We have several services available to fit the needs of any rental owner, and you are free to choose which services you need us to handle on your behalf. Our fees are competi-

tive in the marketplace; we charge a small percentage (10 percent) of the monthly rent as a management fee. Our leasing program's fee to find and place a qualified tenant is 50 percent of the monthly rent, and our lease renewal fee to renew a lease with the current tenant is as low as 20 percent.

There are a lot of property management companies that will advertise lower fees, but they often offer inferior services and have hidden costs. Keep in mind, "There are some who know the price of everything but the value of nothing."

Q: Does (Your Property Management Company) charge extra for overseeing maintenance repairs?
A: No! This is part of our standard service to you, the owner, and it is included in our management fees. We do not accept rebates from vendors, nor do we charge fees to tenants to oversee maintenance repairs.

WHAT ADDITIONAL FACTORS SHOULD YOU, THE OWNER, CONSIDER WHEN EMPLOYING THE SERVICES OF A MANAGEMENT COMPANY?

In this section you will cover some of the key ingredients that will help create the terms of your management agreement. This is important because it will change from client to client. Make sure you use the SEOTA information to help establish realistic guidelines up front; this interview process is extremely important to you and your business. Remember, not all business is good business. You need to determine whether or not managing a prospective client's property or properties is a good fit for them as well as you. Understanding the prospective client's needs and concerns before signing a management agreement can actually save you both time and money.

Sometimes property owners commit to obligations they later regret because they are unfamiliar with evaluating management agreements, or they have not taken sufficient time to review the document. Our practice has been to provide a copy of the management agreement to you for review before setting up a consultation. We want you to see, up front, that there are several ways our management agreement is unique and provides confidence and flexibility to you, the owner.

Management Fees Apply Only When Rent is Collected

- We do not charge management fees when your property is vacant.
- We do not charge management fees on uncollected rent.
- We do not charge owners or tenants administrative fees to oversee maintenance repairs.

In short, your success is important to us. Therefore, we only get paid when you get paid.

We Have an Easy Termination Policy

(Your Property Management Company) agreements are as easy and flexible as you will find anywhere. There are three provisions:

1. If a lease agreement or a move-in cost sheet has not been executed by a tenant, you may terminate our management agreement, in writing, at any time, and the only cost to you is any out-of-pocket expenses related to your property, such as an authorized marketing cost.
2. If the property has been leased, but we have managed the property less than six months, you may terminate our management agreement in writing, with sixty days' notice, and the only cost is a nominal termination fee of three hundred dollars (and management fees incurred during the time we managed the leased property, including the sixty-day notice period for services provided).
3. If the property has been leased and we have managed it for more than six months, you may terminate in writing within sixty days' notice without penalty. The only amount due would be the management fees for the time period our services were provided.

No Management Fees After Termination

Many management agreements stipulate that if you terminate the agreement and the tenant remains in the property, you could owe fees to the former property manager as long as the tenant remains. The (**Your Property Management Company**) management agreement has no such clause. We will assign the lease to you, the owner, or another property manager at no charge. We will only accept payment for the time period that our services were rendered.

FREQUENTLY ASKED QUESTIONS ABOUT QUALIFYING TENANTS, LEASING, RENTS, AND OVERALL RENTAL INVESTMENT MARKET CONDITIONS

One of the major questions that most rental owners have for a property management business is how the management company will market and qualify prospective tenants. By addressing these concerns up front, you not only show that this process is not an issue for your management company but that you have a well-thought-out plan for filling vacancies with qualified tenants. Remember, there is a difference between economic occupancy and physical occupancy. Show the prospective client you understand this concept, and having the systems in place could very well be the competitive advantage you need to build a relationship with the prospective client.

Q: How long will it take to rent a property?

A: There are several factors that influence any given rental market, such as location, condition of the rental unit, rental price, and the demographics and psychographics of the target prospects. Demographics tell us who will rent from us, and psychographics tell us why they rent. (To help our property owners better understand the importance of how to evaluate a target rental area and market, we provide a free seminar that covers how to locate and buy rental property.) Keep in mind that the demand for affordable housing will only continue to increase with such economic indicators as higher interest rates and lower availability of affordable rentals for an increasingly large middle-income population. As a result, the ability to find high-quality tenants will only increase. Typically, the time frame to rent a unit should take no more than thirty to sixty days.

Q: How will (Your Property Management Company) market my rental unit?

A: Getting your property rented as soon as possible by a qualified tenant is one of our highest priorities. Lost rent because of unnecessary vacancies is typically never recovered.

Therefore, we use many methods of advertising to give your property the widest possible exposure. These include, but are not limited to:

- Internet listing sources—we advertise your properties on a broad or targeted list of listing sites, depending on your custom marketing strategy.
- Rental spotlight list—this is useful if you have your own website to feature listings. Your property description will be added to our rental list. This list of available or upcoming rentals is updated daily and available free of charge to all.
- Other real estate offices and rental locator services—this is useful if you have any referral sources. If you are interested, your rental information will be shared with other real estate offices looking to locate rentals for their clients. Additional fees may apply and will vary with each locator service.

Q: How does (Your Property Management Company) qualify prospective tenants?

A: (Your Property Management Company) uses one of the most comprehensive tenant screening services in the nation. Powered by The Landlord Property Management Academy in partnership with TransUnion's SmartMove software, this screening program will evaluate the following areas of a prospective tenant's background:

- Rental records
- Employment verifications
- Court evictions
- Driving record
- Criminal background check
- Retail credit files
- Rental debt collection records

The amount of detail you choose to cover in your screening process will be up to you, though we do have recommended criteria. We can help you create personalized screening criteria. We also recommend that you access the article "Finding a Blue Chip Tenant" on landlordacademy.com. This article will provide a more detailed explanation of the impact of finding a good tenant, while also examining the liabilities a landlord *and* property owner could face if tenants are not properly screened.

Q: How long will it take to qualify an applicant?

A: Depending on the level of screening, the process could take as little as fifteen to twenty minutes, or it could take as long as one business day. Our team is trained in techniques to close a deal quickly, even if approval is still pending.

Q: Does (Your Property Management Company) guarantee your leasing services?

A: We are so confident in our tenant qualification process that we offer the following guarantee to owners: If a tenant qualified by our company breaks the original lease agreement within the first year for any reason, we will waive our customary lease fee and rerent the property to a new tenant for *free*!

Q: What if additional persons move into the rental property during a tenancy?

A: This is a common and costly problem rental owners face. To proactively address this issue, this is prohibited in our lease agreement. If an unauthorized person moves in to any unit, a seven-day notice to cure will be served, requiring this person to move out or be added to the lease—but only after completing an application and being approved through our tenant screening process. This entire process must be completed within seven calendar days. Failure to comply can result in the termination of the lease agreement.

Q: Does the rent stay the same until a tenant moves out?

A: Our management is designed to not only manage the day-to-day activities of your property, but to maximize its cash-flow potential. One key to increasing a property owner's cash flow and the overall value of the property is to periodically increase the rents in accordance with market rates. Approximately six weeks before the end of each lease period, we evaluate the market rent of your property to see how much we should raise the rent in order to keep it in line with the current market conditions. A lease renewal is then presented to the tenant with the new rent amount stipulated. Approximately 80 percent of our tenants accept the new rental rate and renew the lease. Of those who choose to move, it is rarely because of a rent increase. Additionally, it has been our experience that the increase in profits owners receive through rent increases has, over time, more than covered the cost of our management fees. Our team constantly conducts market surveys to maintain the ability to keep pace with current market rent conditions. This includes an evaluation of not only rental amount but also amenities offered and other competitive factors.

Q: What happens if the tenant doesn't pay the rent?

A: This is one of the most frequently asked questions by owners and the subject of greatest concern. When a tenant fails to pay the rent and remains in the rental unit, we begin the process to quickly have the tenant removed. Our trained team knows how to file the required legal notices to prepare for an eviction process. We work closely with premier and experienced eviction attorneys to make sure not only that you receive fast, excellent service, but that you receive those services at a competitive rate. For more details on how an eviction works, please review the eviction time line provided on landlordacademy

.com. Once the eviction is completed in the court system, the tenant is required to physically move from your property. We coordinate the required performance of the writ of possession by a local sheriff, which then puts our management company back in possession of the rental unit. Finally, our trained team handles any abandoned property as required by state law. (Left-behind property is one of the most costly areas of landlording, and it is an issue that can often lead to lawsuits if not handled appropriately.)

Once the eviction process is complete, we quickly make the rental unit ready to show and lease again. In fact, at the time of the initial filing we would have already begun to advertise and find a new tenant. The eviction process usually takes three to four weeks, not months, as many would believe. For our clients, an eviction usually costs the owner an initial legal fee of only $150.

Q: How likely is it that an eviction will occur on my property?
A: Although we can never be 100 percent certain, the superior property management training our staff has received, as well as our industry-leading management systems and tenant screening processes, has been proven to significantly reduce the frequency of evictions, as compared to a property management company that has equivalent training but does not employ our same systems and processes.

WHO IS RESPONSIBLE: THE OWNER OR THE TENANT?

Gaining a clear understanding up front of the responsibilities of both parties is key to building a trusting, successful relationship with your prospective client. Keep in mind that most of the time this subject is never covered until something has gone wrong. To avoid any finger-pointing, it's best to cover in detail with your prospective client who will be responsible for what.

Before we address the most common questions in this category, it is important to note that the amount of owner versus tenant responsibility is typically impacted by the number of rental units on the property. More specifically, tenants in single-family rentals are typically willing to assume more responsibility for maintenance and other matters than residents of multifamily rentals.

What Happens if the Tenant Damages the Property?

After eviction-related questions, this is probably the second-largest area of concern for owners. Because of our comprehensive tenant-screening program, our tenants are ones who consistently pay the rent on time and who also take care of the rental property. In the event the tenants do cause damage, they are instructed to repair the damage at their expense. A follow-up inspection by the property manager will determine if the work has been performed properly. If tenant-caused damages are discovered at the time the tenant vacates the premises, a claim is made against the security deposit to cover the damage. This is a legal process that must be followed precisely to allow deduction of a security deposit. If not handled correctly and within the allowed time frame, the entire security deposit may be required to be returned to the tenant, regardless of damages.

Who Is Responsible for the Heating/Air-Conditioning System?

This is a shared responsibility. The owner is responsible for the major operations of the system when things go wrong that are beyond the control of the tenant. However, the tenant is responsible for changing the filters regularly and keeping the drain line open. System maintenance or repair necessitated by tenant abuse, misuse, or neglect is the responsibility of the tenant. To help our tenants better understand the level of preventive maintenance we expect them to perform, we provide them with a preventive maintenance guide at the move-in meeting that explains in detail various preventive-maintenance techniques.

These responsibilities are also spelled out in our lease agreement.

Who Is Responsible for Plumbing Repairs?

Once again, this is a shared responsibility. Owners are responsible for circumstances beyond the tenant's control, such as water-heater failure, tree roots in the sewer line, or worn-out fixtures. However, the tenant is responsible for clogged toilets or drains; toilet seats, flappers, and handles; jammed garbage disposals; and any problem resulting from abuse, misuse, or neglect. If the premise has a septic tank system, owners are customarily responsible for septic tank pump-outs, sump-pump failure, and clogged drain fields.

Who Is Responsible for Windows and Screens?

The owner is responsible through the property manager to ensure that these are in good condition when the tenant takes possession. After that, the tenant is responsible for the repair or replacement of broken glass or damaged screens, including screen doors and sliding doors. One exception would be if the damage occurred because of a natural disaster such as a major storm.

Who Is Responsible for Pest Control?

Our lease agreement makes this a tenant responsibility for single-family homes and duplexes, except for problems beyond the tenant's control, including termites, carpenter ants, pharaoh ants, and rodents. (Florida statutes stipulate that for multifamily buildings larger than a duplex, pest control must be an owner's responsibility.)

Who Takes Care of the Yard?

Our single-family lease agreement makes this a tenant responsibility and requires the tenant to maintain the yard and shrubs in the same condition the yard was in during move-in, unless the owner chooses to provide complete lawn care for the property.

Many owners now provide a chemical lawn service: a quarterly fertilization, weed control, and insect control treatment for about twenty-five dollars per month.

Hazardous work such as tree trimming is an owner's responsibility and is arranged and scheduled by the property manager. The cost of this service would be the responsibility of the owner and would, thus, need to be preapproved.

Who Is Responsible for Swimming Pool Service?

It has been our experience that it is best for this service to be provided by the owner to make sure that the pool is maintained properly. We contract with a pool service company to provide weekly pool services. The cost of this service would be the responsibility of the owner and would, thus, need to be preapproved.

What Is Your Policy on Animals?

Whether or not to accept animals is always the owner's decision. Some owners allow animals; others do not. A nonrefundable fee of one hundred dollars per animal and an additional two-hundred-dollar security deposit per animal must be paid by the tenant in order to have an animal in the rental unit. Where animals are permitted, only small to medium-sized, nonviolent, common domesticated animals would be considered. Certain breeds of dogs are not accepted because of liability considerations. Farm animals are also not permitted. (Due to fair housing laws, persons with disabilities will be allowed a therapy pet without being charged a pet fee. For more information, please review the Fair Housing Act provided in this manual.)

What Does (Your Property Management Company) Do When the Rental Becomes Vacant?

To reduce out-of-pocket costs to the owner, we promptly conduct a move-out inspection of the rental premises. This allows us to make any appropriate claims against the security deposit for damages made by the tenant and then disburse the deposit accordingly. We then immediately prepare the property for rerent. This process is referred to as the punch-out and typically includes cleaning the carpet, painting the walls, and so on. As soon as we are notified the unit will become vacant, we begin advertising for a new tenant. This is often the best time to address major repairs, improvements, or upgrades to the rental unit if needed.

What Kind of Liability Insurance Should a Property Owner Have?

If you are converting your personal residence to a rental property, you should change your policy from a homeowner's policy to a landlord's policy (sometimes called a rental dwelling or dwelling fire policy). If your property is already a rental unit, you probably have the right policy, but please check just to be sure. The limits should be in an amount not less than $100,000 per person and $300,000 per occurrence.

If your rental property is in a condominium or two-home community, please do not assume that the condo association policy for the community will adequately cover you or your property. It will not! You should have your own liability policy (separate from the association's policy) to make sure that both you and your rental property are adequately protected.

If you do not know an insurance agent, we can recommend local, independent insurance agents who will be glad to recommend the appropriate policy for you.

It is the policy of (**Your Property Management Company**) that you, the owner, request that your insurance company add (**Your Property Management Company**) as an "additional insured" to your policy. Most companies make this addition at no extra charge. Some companies, however, have a policy against adding coverage for management agents to your policy. In theses cases (Your Property Management Company) reserves the right to charge the owner's account once each year a nominal insurance charge (fifty dollars for one house) when we are not covered under the owner's policy as an "additional insured."

What Is (Your Property Management Company)'s Rental Inspection Program?

In addition to overseeing all maintenance and repairs, as well as handling all tenant relations as part of our regular management responsibilities, we can conduct an annual inspection of the visual interior and exterior of a rental property, complete an inspection report, and provide a copy of the report to you, the owner. Due to its complexity, the annual inspection is not a part of our normal management services. But for a reasonable investment of $125, we will gladly perform these very important services.

QUICK TIPS ON HOW TO PREPARE YOUR PROPERTY FOR RENTAL

- Carpet should be professionally cleaned and in good condition with no pet odor.
- Premises, interior and exterior, should be in "move-in clean" condition.
- All windows and sliding glass doors should operate and lock properly, with all screens in good condition.
- All appliances and other systems related to the premises should be clean and in good condition and repair: stove, refrigerator, dishwasher, microwave, garbage disposal, central heat/air system, automatic garage door opener, etc.
- All plumbing fixtures should be in good repair and working properly.
- All bathroom tiles should be in good condition with no loose tile, and tile cracks and corners should be properly caulked or grouted.
- Kitchen and bath countertops and back seams should be properly caulked and splash boards should be in good condition.
- Window treatments (drapes, horizontal blinds, vertical blinds, shades) should be clean and in good working condition.
- All electrical outlets and switches should be in good condition and have cover plates.
- Interior paint should be newly applied.
- Smoke alarms should be properly installed in bedroom areas and in proper working order.
- Household-rated fire extinguisher should be on the premises and properly serviced.
- All light fixtures should have lightbulbs and be in proper working order. Ceiling fans, if any, should be clean and in proper working order.
- Lawn should be clean; grass cut, edged, and trimmed; shrubs trimmed; and irrigation systems (if applicable) in good working order. (This is essential to the "curb appeal" of the property, which directly impacts the speed of leasing.)
- Well-water system and any water softener system, if applicable, should be in good working order, with appropriate chemicals added at proper levels.

- House numbers three inches high should be properly displayed on the front of the house or apartment unit as well as on any street-side mailbox.
- Roof should be in good condition with no leaks.
- All debris, trash, and/or discards should be removed from the rental unit premises, including from the attic.
- All exterior door locks should be changed after the last occupant. Each exterior door should have an entrance lock and a single cylinder dead-bolt lock.
- Exterior paint should have good appearance with no significant fading, chalking, weathering, or peeling.
- Copies of all warranties, service contacts, and termite and/or pest control contracts should be provided to (**Your Property Management Company**).

Your Team (Your Property Management Company)

Insert the names of your team members, their roles or job titles, and contact information here. Designate who is the emergency contact after hours and on weekends, or provide a schedule if that contact rotates.

Be sure to include the CPMS designation and any other certifications these individuals have.

It's also a great idea to include a photo of each team member. This makes an owner feel more at ease when meeting someone at the property for the first time, as well as making the relationship a little more connected.

GOING BEYOND PROPERTY OWNERS' EXPECTATIONS

With our company, you will always have the ability to inspect what you expect from us. This is accomplished many different ways. One common way is through our property management reporting system. In essence, your property's performance can constantly be evaluated with these quick and easy reports.

Now it's time to make your rental portfolio work for you. This is accomplished by allowing (**Your Property Management Company**) to help provide the tools, knowledge, wisdom, and proper alliances necessary to profitably invest in rental property. We do this in many different ways.

One way is to provide constant up-to-date educational courses, consultation, and market reports to act as a guide for those who are new to rental investing. And if you are a veteran investor, think of our company as water—providing you with the ability to adapt by being able to flow in any direction the current or future market may lead us.

MARKETING AND LEASING

As an investor/owner, you can expect our normal leasing services to include the following:

- We will place one of our (**Your Property Management Company**) "Now Leasing" signs on your property (if permitted) as soon as a vacancy is recorded, usually thirty to sixty days early.
- We will place a full voice description of your property in our voice mail system, which provides information to interested renters twenty-four hours a day.
- We will share information with interested renters by using real estate locator services, website full-photo and description advertisements, and curb advertisements. (Additional fees may apply for website and locator services.)

- We will have our trained leasing staff show your property to prospective tenants during rental touring hours.
- During the rental tour, when a prospect decides that they are ready to move forward with leasing, we will immediately ask the prospect to complete our prospect packet, which includes our application. Our team then begins the efficient but comprehensive applicant qualification process. This will ensure we have a qualified tenant and that the security deposit is received by money order or electronic payment for your financial protection. We can usually have a prospective tenant approved within fifteen to twenty minutes of receiving their application.
- We will not rent your property for an amount lower than what you have agreed to without first receiving your permission.
- We will conduct the move-in meeting with the tenant and have the tenant examine and sign a move-in/move-out inspection report. This will ensure the tenant and property manager agree on the condition of the rental unit before the tenant receives the keys. After the move-in/move-out inspection report is signed, we will review and sign the lease, as well as the rules and regulations form, and then turn the keys over to the tenant. This move-in process is a proven method for developing the trust needed for a successful tenant relationship; it also provides the documentation and legal structure necessary to protect the owner if problems occur in the future.

LEASE RENEWALS

As an investor/owner, you can expect our normal procedures to include the following:

Our renewal program will allow us to be proactive in renewing the tenant's lease. We will have evaluated the current rental market to determine how much of an increase the current tenant can expect. If the tenant decides not to renew the lease (which is less than a 20 percent probability, based on our experience), we will be proactive in re-leasing the rental unit at the current market rental rate.

PROPERTY INSPECTION PROGRAM

As an investor/owner, you can expect our normal procedures to include the following:

- Our team will inspect your property at least once each week when it is vacant.
- Our team will go through our Inspect What We Expect Checklist, which consists of walking through the whole rental unit with the move-in/move-out inspection report to detect any damage caused by the tenant who previously moved out. If damages

are found caused by the previous tenant, then we will follow our system to properly impose a claim against the security deposit.

- When authorized by the owner in writing, we will conduct an annual visual interior and exterior inspection of the rental property. After we complete the inspection report, a copy will be made available to the owner. **There is an additional charge of $125 for these services.**

WHY WE ARE THE TOP IN OUR INDUSTRY

As an investor/owner, you can expect our normal procedures to include the following:

(**Your Property Management Company**) will follow a very innovative system model. This system model enables us to provide very dependable and predictable services to our clients. All of our team members have studied and received our distinguished designation as Certified Property Management Specialists™. Our team is required to renew this designation annually and required to complete six continuing education classes in industry-related courses, as provided by The Landlord Academy™.

DAY-TO-DAY OPERATIONS

As an investor/owner, you can expect our normal procedures to include the following:

- Our team will make owning rental property as an investment not only smart but easy. We will make every reasonable effort to collect the rent in a timely fashion. Rent is due on the first of the month and is considered late after the fifth.
- Through our experienced staff and our state-of-the-art property management software, we make responding to all tenant concerns and emergencies quick and efficient.
- Our team will make every reasonable effort to renew the lease with the current tenant with a rent increase that reflects the current market rental rate.

WHAT IF A TENANT DOES NOT COMPLY WITH THE LEASE AGREEMENT OR RULES AND REGULATIONS?

As an investor/owner, you can expect our normal procedures to include the following:

- Our team will serve any applicable legal notice under state law to ensure compliance with the lease agreement.
- Our team will make a follow-up visit to the rental property to determine whether or not the tenant has complied in a timely manner with any and all legal notices or letters delivered by us.
- Our team personally delivers all notices and letters, including the three-day notice.
- Our team also works with the top landlord-tenant and eviction attorneys in Florida. They will assist in any eviction action taken against a delinquent or noncomplying tenant. This procedure will always be done in a timely fashion, unless directed by the owner to allow a delay.

REPORTING TO OWNERS

As an investor/owner, you can expect our normal procedures to include the following:

- Our team will prepare and e-mail or fax a copy of any and all comprehensive statements along with the owner's distribution check no later than the seventeenth day of the month.
- Our state-of-the-art property management software allows for many useful, detailed reports. Our team will fax or e-mail the owner key reports they request once a month.
- We also provide copies of all vendor invoices for expenses charged to your account.
- We will deposit your distribution check directly into your bank account if we have mutually agreed in writing to do so.
- Our team will also send a 1099 income form and profit and loss statement at the end of each calendar year to assist you in your tax preparation.

WHAT ABOUT MAINTENANCE AND UPGRADES?

As an investor/owner, you can expect our normal procedures to include the following:

- Our team will consult with you, the property owner, in advance regarding any expenditure that would exceed $250, **unless it is an emergency affecting the safety or health of the tenant, or the integrity of the property**. We will obtain written permission to proceed with any property expenditure exceeding $250, unless an emergency.
- We will arrange and authorize services necessary to maximize the property's appeal to prospective tenants, thus expediting the leasing process and minimizing vacancy time. Examples would include: utilities, maid service, carpet cleaning, lawn service, pool services, painting, and minor repairs.
- We will change the locks between tenants' residencies to decrease owner's liability.
- We also will only use properly licensed and insured vendors who are highly qualified and have experience dealing with the rental industry to perform the work on your property.

WE COMPLY WITH LOCAL, STATE, AND GOVERNMENTAL REGULATIONS

As an investor/owner, you can expect our normal procedures to include the following:

- We comply with local, state, and federal fair housing laws and ordinances.
- We comply with all state statutes regarding landlord-tenant law.
- We comply with U.S. EPA requirements regarding lead-based paint disclosure.
- We comply with all other applicable laws and ordinances, whether local, state, or federal, that may affect the management of residential rental property.
- We will also make it company policy for all team members to carry the Certified Property Management Specialist™ designation from The Landlord Academy™, an academy recognized on a national level for providing landlord and rental investor courses. This ensures that the aforementioned items are not only understood but carried out.

THE GET-STARTED CHECKLIST

The following is a list of items we will need to begin management of your rental property:

- A signed management agreement by all owners of the property.
- If applicable, a completed lead-based paint hazard disclosure form. This form only applies to homes built before 1978. Disregard this form if your property was built after 1978.
- All keys pertaining to the rental property: house keys, pool keys, garage door opener remotes, and gate entry cards and/or remotes to the community. Four (4) sets of keys are ideal. If you don't have that many keys available, we can make duplicates. For liability and security reasons, if the rental property has been occupied either by the owner or a tenant, all locks should be rekeyed before a new tenant moves in. Please do not duplicate keys unnecessarily.
- A copy of the homeowner association or condo association rules and regulations where your property is located, along with the name and address of the governing association. (Disregard if your property is an apartment complex.)
- A copy of your insurance policy, naming our company as an additional insured. Please return to us written confirmation that our company has been added as an additional insured.
- If applicable, a copy of any current lease agreement and assignment from previous landlord to our company, as well as tenant names and contact information.
- If applicable, security deposits for any existing tenants or written information on where these deposits are being held.
- A completed and signed W-9 form providing your social security number or taxpayer identification number, or other applicable taxpayer form (e.g., W-8, 4224) for non-U.S. citizens.
- A check in the amount of $250 to fund the rental trust account. Please make check payable to (**Your Property Management Company Trust Account**).
- A completed authorization for automatic deposits form with voided check attached, if you wish to have your funds electronically deposited into your bank account each month.

Thank you. We look forward to developing a successful strategic alliance with you!

CONCLUSION

Thank you for allowing us this time to introduce our revolutionary property management company to you. We hope this handbook has helped you better understand how to evaluate a property management company, in addition to providing you with very important industry knowledge. At (**Your Property Management Company**) our main focus is to maximize your income and minimize your expenses through a strategic alliance between you and our team.

We would consider it a privilege to help you continue to grow your real estate portfolio.

Let's Get Started!

To move forward:

1. Please contact us at: (***insert your contact info here***)
2. Begin completing the get-started checklist on page 193.

THE MANAGEMENT AGREEMENT

Your **management** agreement should be comprised of information from your management proposal. It will establish in contract form the relationship between you and the client. This is extremely important in preventing misunderstandings and resolving future disagreements. It is designed to protect both parties and spell out the rules of the game. You must understand all of the terms of your contract in order to protect yourself and to remain in compliance. On the other hand, a poorly crafted management agreement will have the opposite effect. Terms of the management agreement need to accurately reflect the relationship between client and manager. Terms will change from client to client.

Key components for the management agreement should include:

- Key elements of the relationship between the property manager and owner
- Compensations—fee structure and when and how monies are paid
- Statement of each party's responsibilities
- Authority of the manager
- Owner's obligations
- Property manager's obligations

The following is a sample management agreement.

Property Management Agreement

This is a Property Management Agreement, an AGREEMENT between _____, hereinafter referred to as "Owner" and _____, hereinafter referred to as "Agent," who agree as follows:

I. EXCLUSIVE RIGHT TO RENT, LEASE, AND MANAGE:

Owner hereby employs Agent, giving Agent the exclusive right to rent, lease, and manage Owner/Investor/Investor's property (hereinafter called the "Rental Property"), more specifically: _____
_____

Agent accepts the management of the Rental Property for the period, and upon the terms herein provided.

II. TERM:

This Agreement shall commence on _____ and shall end when either Owner or Agent shall give the other party notice of intent to terminate according to terms stipulated in section VII of this Agreement.

III. MANAGEMENT AUTHORITY AND AGENT RESPONSIBILITIES:

Owner expressly grants to Agent the following authority, powers, and rights, any or all of which may be exercised in the name of Owner, in Agent's name alone, or in the names of both, and Owner shall assume all responsibilities for expenses in connection with the managed property, and shall reimburse or pay in advance all expenses incurred or to be incurred by Agent according to this Agreement:

 a. Full management and control of the Rental Property with authority to collect all rent and other monies and securities from Tenants and or Occupants in the Rental Property, and issue receipts for same.

 b. The exclusive right to accept and qualify applications for rental and to perform credit checks and other screening services on applicants, and the exclusive right to approve or decline such applicants. Owner shall not be provided with the Tenants and or Occupants credit report and/or application unless specifically authorized in writing by the tenant and the provider of the credit report.

 c. To prepare and negotiate new leases and renewals of existing leases in which Agent is authorized to execute leases and renewals for a maximum of one calendar year or for extended periods with Owner/Investor/Investors' approval.

 d. To have repairs made to the property, to purchase necessary supplies, to provide for all negotiation and contractual arrangements by suppliers or other independent contractors for all improvements, maintenance, or repair services deemed necessary by Owner and/or Agent or to comply with applicable building, housing, and health codes, and to determine that such services were performed in an acceptable manner. On each improvement, maintenance, or repair item that shall exceed $_____ dollars ($) in cost—except for emergency repairs—Owner's approval shall first be obtained.

 e. To change or replace locks on Rental Property between tenancies.

 f. To place "For Rent" signs on the Rental Property unless prohibited by applicable bylaws or local ordinances.

 g. To advertise the Rental Property when vacant or in anticipation of vacancy.

 h. Advertise on websites not to exceed a budget approved in advance by Owner.

 i. To serve any and all applicable legal notices to Tenants and/or Occupants and to prosecute legal actions to terminate tenancies, evict Tenants and/or Occupants, and recover rents and any other fees due, and when necessary hiring or consulting for these issues a reputable attorney.

j. To collect from Applicants or Tenants and or Occupants any or all of the following: application fees, late rent fees, nonnegotiable check fees, re-leasing fees, lease modification fees, legal notice services fees, or any other fees that may now or in the future become a Tenant obligation. All such fees shall belong to Agent to offset Agent's extra time and expense for handling additional work and responsibilities related to such fees, and Agent need not account for such fees to Owner. First funds collected from Tenant each month shall be applied to Tenant obligations chronologically beginning with the earliest obligation incurred. Any outstanding Tenant obligations at end of tenancy may be deducted from Tenant's security deposit and/or last month's rent.

k. To resolve disputes over security deposits and any other fees due. Agent may use any lawful means to resolve such disputes. Agent is authorized to compromise and settle claims on Owner's behalf as may be necessary or prudent in Agent's judgment.

l. To accept or decline checks for rental and other payments due from Tenants and or Occupants according to Agent's policies. Agent shall not be held liable for bad checks or money not collected. Owner shall reimburse Agent for any fees disbursed on the faith of such checks should they be uncollectible for any reason. Owner agrees to hold Agent harmless for any failure to secure Tenants and/or Occupants for the Owner, any cancellation by the Tenants and/or Occupants and/or failure to collect any rents or monies due from the Tenants and/or Occupants for any reason.

m. To make every reasonable effort to collect rents and other monies from Tenant when and as they become due; however, Agent does not guarantee the payment of Tenant obligations. Agent may employ collection agencies, attorneys, or any other reasonable and lawful means to assist in the collection of any outstanding Tenant obligation.

n. To render monthly statements to Owner of income and expenses and to disburse to Owner the net proceeds of such accounting.

o. Statements shall be provided between the 17th and 20th day of each month.

p. To deposit all receipts collected for Owner or held on behalf of Tenant in escrow accounts separate from Agent's personal funds. However, Agent shall not be held liable in the event of bankruptcy or failure of depository (such as a bank or banking institution.) Agent may require releases from all parties in the event of a controversy before disbursing escrow funds.

q. To receive interest on any Agent escrow accounts, and interest received, if any, above that which may be required by state law to be paid to Tenant or others, shall belong to Agent to offset Agent's time and expenses of maintaining such accounts, and Agent need not account for such interest received to Owner.

r. To arrange for authorized individuals to inspect, survey, or view the Rental Property as directed by Owner.

s. To provide security deposit evaluations to Owner and submit recommendations and cost estimates, if any, to Owner at the expiration of a tenancy.

t. To honor Owner's preference with respect to allowing pets to be kept on the Rental Property. Pets—other than animals trained or used for assisted living purposes—will be permitted only with prior approval of Owner.

u. Agent is vested with such other general authority and power as may be necessary or expedient to carry out the spirit and intent of this Agreement. Agent assumes no responsibility for any other services unless agreed to in writing.

v. Rental Rates will be the current market rate as determined in the sole judgment of Agent but no less than $ _____ per month. Late charges or fees owed by any Tenants and/or Occupants shall be collected at the discretion of the Agent and Agent shall retain any such charges and late fees.

w. Agent is given the authority to sign all lease(s).

x. Damages or Missing Items: Agent is not responsible for damage to the Rental Property or items missing, switched out, lost, or damaged under any circumstances, including but not limited to theft, vandalism, or negligence of Tenants and or Occupants or their guests. In furnished units, an inventory will be checked by Agent at departure. In the event Tenants and/or Occupants damage the Rental Property or owe any monies to the Owner, Agent is given the exclusive authority to determine in its professional judgment the amount due, charge the Tenants and or Occupants accordingly, and/or settle with the Tenants and/or Occupants upon advice of Agent's legal counsel. Agent is given the power to make claims upon the security deposit on behalf of Owner and Agent shall not be held liable for any failure to make claims on any damages which were not readily apparent to Agent.

IV. OWNER/INVESTOR/INVESTORS PROVIDES THE FOLLOWING ASSURANCES:

a. That the Rental Property is owned by Owner. Owner will provide a copy of the deed if requested by Agent. That Owner has full power and authority to hire Agent and has the right to receive income proceeds from the Rental Property and that this power, authority, and right have not been assigned or transferred to others.

b. That all mortgages, taxes, insurances, and association dues are currently paid and are not in default, and that the Rental Property is not now the subject of a foreclosure or pending foreclosure action. In the event a foreclosure action is filed against Owner, Agent shall be notified immediately in writing. Owner shall indemnify, defend, and hold Agent harmless in any foreclosure action.

V. OWNER/INVESTOR/INVESTORS ACCEPTS THE FOLLOWING RESPONSIBILITIES:

a. To keep Agent informed of any changes of Owner's interest in the Rental Property.

b. To be responsible for payment of the following recurring expenses: mortgage payments, taxes, fire or other insurance premiums, Homeowner/Investor/Investors/Condominium Association obligations, and any other recurring expenses unless that responsibility has been accepted by Agent in writing. Agent shall not be required to advance its own money to pay any Owner's obligations, including recurring expenses, unless Owner has provided sufficient funds to cover the amount. Monthly income collected, if any, shall be applied chronologically beginning with the earliest obligation, including Agent's compensation, and the remaining balance, if any, shall be available for remaining obligations and recurring expenses. Mailing of previous month's statement to Owner shall be sufficient notice to Owner of balance on hand and the need for additional funds. Owner assumes full responsibility for any consequences resulting from late payment or nonpayment of any obligation or recurring expenses should Agent be unable to make said payments due to insufficient funds on hand, lack of income from the Rental Property, nondelivery or delay of mail, or for any other reason beyond Agent's control.

c. To provide Agent with current and up-to-date copies of any applicable Condominium or Homeowner/Investor/Investors Association rules and regulations. In the event Tenants and or Occupants fail to comply with the rules and regulations and the Association or Board levies fees, fines, or assessments against Owner, Agent shall not be liable for the payment of such obligations.

d. To keep Rental Property adequately insured, and shall immediately notify Agent/Property Manager in writing should insurance lapse.

e. To keep Agent informed in writing of any changes of Owner's mailing address and phone numbers.

f. To place in reserve with Agent **two hundred fifty dollars ($250.00)** per property/unit, or such other amount as may be jointly agreed to by Owner and Agent, for the purpose of maintenance, repairs, or other expenses that may arise, and authorize Agent to replenish this reserve from rents collected.

g. To cooperate fully with Agent in complying with all applicable building, housing, and health codes, as well as applicable Fair Housing regulations. **The Rental Property shall be rented without regard to race, creed, color, religion, sex, national origin, age, disability, marital status, familial status, or sexual preference.**

h. To indemnify, defend, and hold Agent harmless to all cost, expenses, suits, claims, liabilities, damages, proceedings, or attorney's fees. Also included, but not limited to, are those arising out of any injury or death to any person or persons or damage to any property of any kind whatsoever. In addition to the above stated would be whomsoever belonging, including Owner, in any way relating to the rental, leasing, and management of the Rental Property or the performance or exercise of any of the duties, obligations, powers, rights, or authority granted to Agent. Owner agrees to and does hereby indemnify and hold harmless the Agent and its employees, and assigns from any and all claims, lawsuits, damages, costs, losses, and expenses arising from the management of the property and from any injury to persons and/or property occurring on or about the Rental Property. Owner agrees to indemnify Agent for damages suffered as a result of any lapse in or failure by Owner to maintain insurance coverage.

i. To carry, at Owner's expenses, such general liability, property damage, and worker's compensation insurance as shall be adequate to protect the interest of both Agent and Owner. Such policies shall name Agent as well as Owner as the party insured, and Owner shall provide Agent with a copy of insurance policy within fourteen (14) days of the execution of this Agreement. Additionally, Agent may carry insurance sufficient to protect Agent's interest solely and shall charge to Owner's Rental Property ten dollars ($10.00) for each additional Rental Property managed by Agent to cover cost of such insurance. Agent may waive this charge with copy of certificate of insurance policy from Owner showing adequate insurance coverage and Agent named as an additional insured.

j. That Agent shall not be liable for any willful neglect, abuse, or damage to Rental Property by Tenants and/or Occupants or others nor for loss of or damage to any personal property of Owner by Tenant including loss due to exchange or theft by Tenants and/or Occupants or others. Agent shall not be responsible for nonpayment of or theft of any utility service by Tenant. Agent shall not be held liable for any error of judgment or mistake of law except in cases of willful misconduct or gross negligence.

k. Utilities: If allowed by law and unless otherwise agreed to by the parties, Tenants and/or Occupants are required to have telephone service, cable, electric service, water service, and all other utilities in their own name. In any lease where the Tenants and/or Occupants shall have use of the Owner's utilities and be responsible for all or part of the bills, Owner shall pay the entire bill in a timely manner and forward copies to this office for reimbursement. Under no circumstances shall Owner cause the termination of these services and Owner agrees to indemnify Agent for any damages or litigation fees/cost incurred by Agent if Owner improperly terminates a utility services. Agent will deduct bills to the extent of funds available and Owner agrees that Agent shall be in no way responsible for nonpayment of or theft of any utility service by Tenants and or Occupants.

VI. MANAGEMENT COMPENSATION: In consideration of the services to be rendered by Agent, Owner shall pay Agent each month any and all of the following forms of compensation as may be applicable as they become due:

a. FOR MANAGEMENT: Ten percent (10%) of the gross monthly rents collected. Should a security deposit claim be made to cover any unpaid rent, management fees will be applicable to such rent also.

b. FOR LEASING: A leasing fee in the amount of 50% of the rent due at the beginning of each new tenancy.

c. LEASING GUARANTEE: If Tenant has been qualified by Agent and defaults on the original lease term, Agent will re-lease the Rental Property and waive the leasing fee (as long as default was without Owner's approval).

d. RENEWALS: A renewal fee of 20% of the rent due upon the renewal of lease. Any extension of the Tenant occupancy shall be deemed a renewal of the previous rental term for the purpose of renewal compensation.

VII. TERMINATION:

a. Either Owner or Agent may terminate this Agreement by giving the other party sixty (60) days' written notice of termination. Agent may terminate this Agreement immediately with written or verbal notice if Owner's actions or inactions appear to be illegal, improper, or jeopardize the safety or welfare of Tenants and/or Occupants or others. Should Owner terminate this Agreement before Agent has managed the Rental Property at least six months, Owner shall pay Agent a termination fee of three hundred dollars ($300.00) or 30 percent of monthly rent, whichever is greater.

b. Owner may terminate this Agreement in writing before Agent/Property Manager has committed to a Tenant for the Rental Property and shall reimburse Agent for any out-of-pocket expenses.

c. All provisions of this Agreement that indemnify, defend, and hold Agent harmless to any and all matters shall survive any termination of this Agreement.

d. Agent may withhold funds for thirty (30) days after the end of the month in which this Agreement is terminated to pay any obligations; Owner shall pay Agent the deficit within thirty (30) days of termination date.

e. In the event this Agreement is terminated by either Owner or Agent, regardless of cause, the parties agree that Agent shall have no further obligation to rent, lease, or manage the Rental Property.

VIII. MODIFICATION OF THIS AGREEMENT:

Agent may change the terms of this Agreement by giving ninety (90) days' written notice to Owner/Investor/Investors. The ninety (90) days shall be counted from the date notice was mailed. Should no written objection be forthcoming from Owner within the ninety (90) day period, Owner's acceptance of said changes shall be presumed. Any exception would be a change required by applicable statute or regulation in which case the change would become effective according to the time period required by such statute or regulation.

Agreed and Signed:

_____

Owner
Name:
Date:

_____

Agent
Name:
Date:

PART III

BUILDING WEALTH WITH PROPERTY MANAGEMENT

LEGAL ASPECTS OF PROPERTY MANAGEMENT

Behind the scenes of operating a property management business

Note: I have written at length about the need for you to protect yourself legally, and I do recommend hiring a local attorney who is knowledgeable about the landlord-tenant laws in your state. In the meantime, though, I did want to provide some additional real estate legal advice that is specific to property management. This chapter is brought to you by attorney Theresa Morelli. She began practicing law in Ohio in 1989 and then served as lead in-house counsel at Forest City Residential Management in Cleveland from 1998 to 2015. Since leaving Forest City, Morelli has been in solo practice with a focus on residential property management law. Here she shares tips and best practices gleaned from more than twenty years in the industry.

When I represented tenants from 1991 to 1997 as a young legal services lawyer, the rental housing landscape was far calmer. When I first began working at Forest City Residential Management in 1998 until about 2006, I saw a significant increase in tenants across the country filing lawsuits, as well as administrative, fair housing, and other complaints with federal, state, and local regulatory agencies. Then, I saw a great rise after 2006. I coined a new term for it: *resident rage.*

Resident rage is at an all-time high. Not only are tenants filing even more lawsuits and administrative complaints, they are mirroring the overall decline of civility in our society. I could fill pages with my own experiences of tenants (ranging from highly affluent professionals and business owners all the way to extremely low-income tenants) acting in unwelcome, unwanted, offensive, and hostile ways to other tenants, the landlord's employees, and to third parties such as other tenants' guests and deliverypersons. Just a few examples are a tenant driving his car into the management office, a much younger tenant placing extremely lewd and lascivious notes under an older tenant's door, a tenant going on multiple websites and blogs and accusing the property manager of killing at least a dozen tenants with toxic black mold, and so much more. One tenant who had filed multiple lawsuits and administrative complaints during her tenancy once e-mailed me that I was Satan's proudest spawn.

So what is the biggest takeaway for property managers, other than to have very thick skin? Today's property managers must have regular training in conflict management and resolution, including but not limited to defusing everyday conflict, dealing with difficult people—especially "high-conflict" individuals, to use the term coined by the author and lawyer William Eddy—understanding different generations and cultures, and learning how to spot burnout and compassion fatigue in their colleagues and themselves. Following are some best practices:

DEALING WITH DIFFICULT PEOPLE AND PREVENTING BURNOUT

- Supervisors and senior leadership must really care about employees and invest in them continually with training and time. It cannot be a facade.
- Dealing with difficult people and preventing burnout both take regular training, whether done on-site, at an annual company meeting or event, or via a bigger company's training and development department. With periodic webinars, video conference calls, and other technology, any company can do this. About external trainers, use the same principles as you would to vet an attorney. Big industry groups also have training conferences, but they are usually not for lower-level employees.
- Care about all employees at all levels. Think about it: The maintenance technicians, housekeepers, custodians, groundskeepers, and so forth are really the people who interact most with the tenants. Train them! Also, failing to train them sends such a disheartening message to them. Be sure to train them in their native languages.
- Many times, people in corporate or regional offices either do not care about employee feelings and/or have no mechanism other than "Call the EAP." I have had senior leadership tell me, "If X cannot handle property management, let them leave and good riddance." Good people get overwhelmed and leave. So, how does that help a company that is already understaffed and not training enough? My direct report, a corporate counsel, and I became trusted business advisors and we often had employees tell us personal things safely. If someone or the other employees or tenants would face harm, I went to HR and to senior leadership. In some cases our advice was heeded and in other cases not. Give employees someone to talk to, but make sure the intermediary is sensitive and confidential and will work for resolutions that benefit all.
- Keep abreast of all ways that difficult tenants express themselves: on social media via Facebook, rating sites, and even their own websites; in nasty e-mails; on nasty calls

and voice mails; in in-person interactions; and by recording without consent the audio and video of interactions and sending to others or posting on sites like YouTube. Train employees and senior leadership on how to communicate effectively and how to defuse angry tenants. I have read books by the lawyer and author William Eddy and he gives very good examples.

- Vet communication professionals the same way you would a lawyer. My suggestion is to focus on two things: (1) dealing effectively with everyday conflict, and (2) knowing when to stop communications and engage lawyers because the tenant's behaviors are not only unwelcome/unwanted/hostile/offensive but also personal, and are an attack based on race, color, sex or gender, national origin, ethnicity, disability status, religion, familial status, or other factors. Involve law enforcement and the court system when tenant behaviors become a direct threat to the health or safety of others—such as getting civil protection orders for threatened employees or sending out "no trespass" notices.

- Provide meaningful on-boarding. Some companies do not do that and expect supervisors to do that with a scrawny checklist. Again, technology affords webinars and online training modules for any company. Still, the most effective training is training on-site by supervisors and peer mentors.

- Be proactive and be ready before problems surface and give employees tools ahead of time. I had employees call me and I had to deal reactively. I then created proactive training. This is ongoing, of course, as challenges continue. My best success was when the bedbug epidemic hit our country's East Coast and Midwest around 2005. I was told by someone I respected in senior leadership that he thought I was crazy when I asked the company to create a bedbug protocol with the timeliest procedures, employee training, and forms for tenants to use. We all saw what happened. A local judge praised the company's bedbug protocol as the most extensive in the country. Some employees did not follow it, of course, yet they had the tools they needed, unlike a lot of other companies' employees—which is true to this day.

THE BIGGEST—AND MOST COSTLY—PROPERTY MANAGEMENT MISTAKE

If I had to pick one misconception that breaks a business, it's that a company (even a very large company) can put its head in the sand about failing to maintain their physical facilities. They want to save pennies, but those pennies literally turn into hundreds of thousands of dollars, to millions, for proper maintenance that has been deferred for years or decades. Add environmental noncompliance to that and you have a business that breaks or is close to breaking for something entirely preventable with foresight and discipline.

My mantra for property maintenance: Completely repair things for functioning now and for better functioning and less costly repairs in the future. Applying Band-Aids and patches will cost you a lot in the future when repairs become very costly and your reputation is sullied. At worst, residents can file their own lawsuits or band together and file class-action lawsuits depending on the nature of the conditions and repairs needed.

Here are some other tips:

- Create a checklist based on the state local building and housing codes, landlord duties under the state/local landlord-tenant laws, any regulations applicable to HUD-assisted housing if the rental housing is HUD-assisted, any regulations applicable to housing choice vouchers if the renter has such a voucher, and any applicable federal regulations based on the age of the housing such as lead-based laws for pre-1978 housing and asbestos laws for pre-1980 housing. High-quality environmental consultants and residential property management lawyers can research such information.
- Do the same for any federal, state, or local accessibility codes or other legal requirements for tenants and visitors with disabilities. High-quality accessibility consultants and residential property management lawyers can research such information. I have seen federal and state agencies require modifications (exterior and interior) costing from the low to high five figures.
- Each rental housing community (by this I mean high-rises, garden/town home apartments, or a privatized military housing by neighborhood) needs to have its own operations and maintenance manual at a minimum. Consult federal, state, and local laws for other requirements depending upon property type and age (e.g., a high-rise built in 1950 with known lead-based paint hazards needs a lead-based paint maintenance plan).
- Deal swiftly with all repairs and maintenance needs. Do so especially with indoor air quality (mold, water intrusion, etc.) and bedbugs. They do not get better on their own; they worsen quickly.
- Train all levels of employees involved in maintenance: dispatchers, groundskeepers, custodians, housekeepers, technicians, managers, etc. Also, if English is their second language, train them with reading and video materials and in-person training taught in their primary language.
- Ideally, have an in-house team of senior leadership with deep experience, high-quality skills, professional certifications and designations from reputable organizations and schools, and tough skin to deal with the "no money to do that" refrains. The senior leadership needs at least one high-level environmental scientist and others with degrees and backgrounds in engineering, construction, and much more. Skimping in this area will result in lawsuits, reputational damage, and federal, state, or local regulatory complaints, all the way to enforcement actions. If your in-house

team lacks basic knowledge and even competence, how will it effectively oversee environmental consultants, contractors, and more? The result is that mistakes and shortcuts taken by contractors, consultants, and other third parties are not detected until the problem is advanced and/or a regulatory agency is contacted by a tenant or unhappy former employee.

- Don't forget to address hazardous conditions created by tenants who kill others/ commit suicide in apartments, deceased tenants found by others or employees, meth labs, ignored pest infestation, ignored unreasonably unsanitary conditions such as human and animal waste, and safety violations by hoarders.

DO YOU NEED TO PUT AN ATTORNEY ON RETAINER?

This is an important question for new business owners who are still growing their incomes and looking to cut costs where possible. And my answer is this: Property managers do not have to put an attorney on retainer to ensure they are following the laws, assuming they take these steps *first*:

- Have an experienced property management attorney review leases and lease-related documents as well as resident selection criteria for compliance with applicable federal, state, and local housing laws, dependent upon the housing type (such as senior housing, market rate housing, affordable housing). Better yet, have such an attorney write them in the first place.
- Have an experienced property management attorney train the client's employees on fair housing compliance, accessibility compliance, state/local landlord-tenant law compliance, and, if applicable, affordable housing compliance for landlords operating federal, state, or local housing assistance programs (such as HUD's Section 8 and 202 programs and the IRS's Section 42 LIHTC program).
- Have an experienced property management attorney and high-quality environmental consultant review the operations and maintenance programs and manuals. They should also review compliance for issues in pre-1978 housing for lead-based paint and other applicable environmental conditions—dependent upon the age of the housing and whether it was built on top of environmentally comprised ground, such as a Superfund site.

For tenancy terminations and other issues with tenants, a prudent landlord/property manager finds an experienced property management attorney who is a trusted advisor and who resolves problems quickly rather than letting them develop into protracted lawsuits and fair housing complaints before HUD and equivalent state/local enforcement agencies.

While most landlords/property managers hire attorneys to do the transactional work, such as affordable housing finance and the purchase/sale agreements, some erroneously assume that operating and managing rental housing is "simple and common sense," so they can save money and delegate legal and regulatory compliance to on-site staff and supervisors. I have found the results to be catastrophic, especially as they relate to lack of environmental compliance. Employees do not learn fair housing compliance from an online module when they are hired, or an occasional class taught by a non-lawyer; they learn it from interacting with and getting regular training from an experienced property management lawyer.

SO HOW DO YOU FIND AN EXPERIENCED PROPERTY MANAGEMENT ATTORNEY?

- Do not hire based on low cost and/or quicker turnaround through the use of clerical assistants and paralegals who do most of the work. Unfortunately, I have seen lawyers let support staff do the paperwork and even deal with clients. I have seen minor to serious errors as a result because support staff, especially, do not understand complex landlord-tenant laws, HUD housing assistance programs, and complicated factual scenarios. Ask the prospective lawyer or law firm who does the actual work, and ask whether there is attorney supervision of the final product. Yes, I have been lied to by outside counsel and I later terminated the lawyer's or the firm's future representation. This type of lawyer or firm is called an "eviction mill" or "eviction services." Avoid them if you want high-quality work and a much lesser chance of losing in court or being subjected to discrimination complaints for the bad advice they gave. The old adage is so true for lawyers: You get what you pay for.
- Ask about the percentage of their practice devoted to landlord-tenant law and fair housing law, and if you operate any HUD or IRS housing programs, ask about that percentage, too. If landlord-tenant law is a sideline or one of many practice areas, the lawyer is not going to be able to handle much but simple evictions for nonpayment of rent or holdover evictions. Anyone with over fifty rental housing units should be using someone whose entire practice, or at least 50 percent of it, is devoted to residential property management law.
- You can check local associations of apartment owners for references, or call others you know in the rental housing industry for references. Some lawyers or law firms have a "lock" in some cities, counties, and even states. Sometimes I found them to be good, but more often than not, they had done a lot of schmoozing with the associations and were not high-quality lawyers. They were better at marketing themselves than handling difficult legal problems effectively.

- Definitely check out prospective lawyers on LinkedIn and find their online presence to see what reported cases they have, what presentations they have given, and whether they have articles and other items shared with the public and prospective clients. Some also are on YouTube and Twitter.
- To me, the ideal property management lawyers have worked in the rental housing industry in-house (which means they really understand management and operational issues). If that's not available, former Legal Aid or Legal Services lawyers are good options, as they have litigated against landlords and will keep you compliant so you do not lose in court. They are often passionate "housing lawyers."
- Ask for sample leases, addenda, and tenancy termination notices. I know that a layperson may not know when a document is not compliant, but I can tell what compliant documents look like. If a lawyer has forms that look generic and cookie cutter even to a layperson, listen to your gut and question your prospective attorney.
- Lawyers can be very good at schmoozing to get business. Ask about turnaround times, whether they look at tenancy files before filing an eviction case or other type of lawsuit (good ones do!), how much work is done by them versus any junior lawyers, and if they bill for each e-mail, text, and phone call. I do not bill for anything under fifteen minutes. Legal bills can be high when lawyers bill for any and all contact.
- My final tip is: What does your gut say about this person? Does the lawyer appear to want to be a true business partner who will work to de-escalate legal issues so they are resolved more quickly and economically? Or will this lawyer be one to drag out things and even encourage litigation for the sake of running up the fees? I have been duped by sweet talkers in the past. Some lawyers, though, will be forthright and tell you that they are aggressive and will do what is necessary to win. I love hiring someone who uses the law and facts. I do not want to hire someone who just files motions to see if the other side will back down.

PROPERTY MANAGEMENT FREQUENTLY ASKED QUESTIONS

We've gone through a lot in this book, so much so that I'm sure you've got the pages highlighted and dog-eared all over the place. And that's good! That means you're learning everything you need to build a business that can impact your family for generations to come. No matter how much information I share, though, I know there's always something else I didn't cover. So in the interest of covering all of my bases, I've included some of the most frequent questions I get asked when I speak at seminars and workshops, along with their answers.

Don't see your question here? Hit me up at bryan@landlordacademy.com and I'll be sure to get back to you!

Q: How did you start in property management, making the leap from an employee working for a property manager to becoming the property manager and now such a successful businessman, author, and speaker?
A: First and foremost it took a lot of motivation—as in, I had to get out of the house! My initial career goal was to play professional basketball, but my dad told me that in the meantime, I had to get a job and a place to live. I was literally hanging with my friend Dwayne in my backyard, telling him how Pops was trying to get me out of the house and how I needed to get a job ASAP. So Dwayne and I walked to the corner store and grabbed a bag of chips and a *Tampa Tribune* to look for employment in the classified ads. There wasn't much that interested me in the newspaper, but I had also picked up an apartment guide and saw a lot of ads for leasing jobs, and some included free housing as part of the compensation. Jackpot!

I didn't have a résumé at the time, so my friend created one for me that was slightly embellished to make sure I stood out among all the applicants. I then faxed it out to every listing from the apartment guide. I immediately started getting calls, and I ultimately landed a job making seven dollars per hour helping with property management as a leasing agent. I had no experience, but with my new job I was finally able to placate my dad. I had an income and a roof over my head.

While my professional basketball window closed, the window to the world of real estate flew wide open. Although I had no experience, I charmed my bosses and knocked their socks off. That first job was difficult because the property management company seemed to have even less experience than I did. I was managing 1,020 units with no property management manual or software tools like we have today, and through that process I learned everything about what not to do. But I pressed on.

In my second job I had a manual and software tools, and to top it off, that job introduced me to the local apartment association and the president of the organization. I must have made a good impression, because he hired me to teach his certified property management program. I became the teacher! This gave me the chance to travel around, speaking to different groups, and to work with the Bay Area Apartment Association. And as I worked and saw how much money the owners of these properties were making, I knew I wanted to start my own business. I eventually moved up the ladder to the management team and then acquisition specialist, but I wanted more.

I started approaching real estate investment clubs for more teaching opportunities. Then, after someone told me that if I wanted to reach the masses I needed to put my information in a book, I wrote a step-by-step manual about how to manage properties. I felt it was my calling to teach others through the systems I developed through hands-on experience.

I sold my manuals out of the trunk of my car—a car that was on its last legs. I kept going around teaching my system, and despite being a horrible speaker at the time, I kept going because I knew the information was totally different from anything else on the market. Eventually my teaching and manual took off, ultimately leading to the development of my first real estate training program, Landlording 101, which eventually morphed into The Landlord Property Management Academy—a full-blown consulting, coaching, and online educational platform designed to help real estate managers and professionals. This evolution all started with the goal of teaching people how to run their own businesses.

Q: You had a head start, but I'm new to real estate. How long will it take me to become successful as a property manager?
A: When I got started in property management, I did already have experience and an influential network, but I am adamant about the fact that even the average person with no experience and no contacts can build a successful property management company. Like anything worth having, it will take hard work and some hustle, but it is possible.

Regarding time frame, it varies from person to person. But I will say this: Right now, I'm sure you know at least one person who is surfing the web, trying to find an online, two-year degree program so they can "get an education and get a good job." Well, I will tell you that in the same amount of time it takes for that individual to get that two-year degree—if you apply everything you've read in this book—your company will be grossing six figures per year. That's my pledge.

Q: What are the start-up costs to become a professional property manager?

A:
- Insurance for your said business will cost approximately two thousand dollars. A real estate license is approximately two thousand to start, but it varies from state to state.
- For tools, I recommend a minimum of a laptop, smartphone, and a tablet computer (the touch screen makes it easy to sign documents electronically), which can add up to another two thousand.
- For building and staffing your business with a receptionist, accountant, and others, you can save a considerable amount of money by using the recommended apps and software outlined earlier. (I also cover best practices for leveraging technology in your business at landlordacademy.com.) These fees will vary based on your specific needs, but they should average around three hundred dollars per month, total.
- Real estate education and training courses can cost up to two thousand dollars.
- Memberships in real estate and investment associations (great for networking and finding client prospects!) will cost between two hundred and five hundred per month, at minimum.
- Finally, for the incorporation of your business, plan for approximately two hundred dollars, depending on your state.

Q: I understand your position on marketing my business by becoming a thought leader, but I still need to know: What are some practical ways to meet investors face-to-face who will hire me to manage their properties?

A: If you are coming from a real estate profession, you will have to shift your mentality from a salesperson to an investor mentality. Find a common denominator and meet a few people doing what you are seeking to do, and then bring your unique strengths to the table. When I first started in property management, I leveraged my knowledge on how to manage assets. Then, I became a client advisor by showing how I could take an investor from point A to point B. Iron sharpens iron, and successful people want to be around other successful people. You've got to get out of the sales mentality and think like an investor.

Q: Can you be a property manager while working a full-time job in a completely different industry?

A: Thanks to today's technology, the answer is: Absolutely! Everything you do can be done from your smartphone, and the execution of many of these routine management tasks will continue to improve and get easier.

Q: Can I be a property manager without hiring staff?
A: Yes! This piggybacks off the previous question, and the online program we provide at landlordacademy.com/30daybiz/ will help your business in thirty days. The smartphone has also taken the new entrepreneur staff to a whole new level. Before, you had to hire an actual receptionist, but now you can accomplish the same tasks with plug-ins. This gives single-owner-operated businesses the illusion of being a big business. And the best part is that as your business continues to grow, you can keep adding plug-ins. We even offer loyalty discounts to some of the plug-in businesses we work with, which you will find on the website.

Q: As a property manager, what protection do I have if the owner of the property I am managing goes into foreclosure?
A: This changes from state and state, but no matter where your business is, make sure you address this in your management agreement with explicit details on what would happen in that situation.

Q: What's the biggest mistake you've made as a real estate entrepreneur and what did you learn from the experience to avoid doing again?
A: Ouch—I remember this well. The biggest mistake I made on the investment side was not fully understanding the purchase side. I did my due diligence on the property, but I did not do my due diligence on the banknote to protect me. When you invest in a property, be sure to carefully read the agreement between you and the bank—especially the small print—to prevent your being left holding a very expensive bag.

Q: As a property manager, how do you set boundaries between your professional time and personal time, especially if there are property emergencies?
A: Leverage the plug-ins I keep discussing, but also leverage your relationships with your contractors—especially in case of an emergency. Make sure you have an emergency hotline in place for your tenants. If you do not have a list of contractors, visit your local Angie's List and Pro Referral. Then, a software program like Ruby Receptionist can take these calls and streamline the communication process to prevent you from being chained to your desk and smartphone 24/7.

Q: Do you need a college degree or certification to be a property manager?

A: You don't need a college degree, but you do need a real estate and broker's license. I also highly recommend the property management designation we offer at our academy.

Q: Can you be a property manager if you have a foreclosure or short sale in your credit history?
A: Yes, your personal credit has no bearing on your ability to start a property management business. And if you have had a foreclosure or bankruptcy, don't let that stop you. No risk, no gain.

Q: How do I overcome my fear of failure—especially financial failure—and take the leap to become a property manager?
A: Believe in yourself! For me it boils down to faith. All of us have God-given talents and each of us has a purpose if we choose to manifest our calling. I truly believe this and chose to take the less secure route in building my business, as I'd rather be broke but living out my life's purpose than making money building someone else's dream. When I am pursuing my dreams and aspirations, I have no regrets. So I say to you, take the risk. That is what God instructed us to do. It is your responsibility to go out and claim everything that God has laid aside for you, and there are no words to describe the tremendous regret you will feel if you reach your deathbed without having ever claimed everything this life has for you. I believe the richest place in the entire world is the graveyard. Every day, million-dollar ideas, cures for diseases, bestselling books, and other great inventions go to the grave with people who had little faith in themselves and the God who filled them with their gifts and talents. If you believe that you have been called to property management, go after it and don't let anything or anyone hold you back!

Q: I attended one of your landlord academies in Miami and wanted to know how your dyslexia/ADHD has impacted, if at all, your success as a property manager, speaker, and author?
A: Yes, my ADHD has played a major role in my success, namely because by pursuing my passions, I was able to build a business around my strengths. If I had not chosen this route, I would have been stuck in a nine-to-five desk job with my weaknesses exposed, and I most likely would have fallen.

Q: Where do you forecast the property management business ten, twenty, and thirty years from now?
A: I forecast it being exactly where it is now—as steady and constant as it has been for over two thousand years. I'll say it again: property management is the cornerstone of real estate. It has always been here, and it will always be here.

Q: I am retiring after thirty-five years in engineering and am considering going into property management for supplemental income and to keep active. What are your suggestions so that my golden years are not stressful?

A: It depends on the asset you choose, whether it is a luxury property (Class A) or middle- to low-income (Class C or D). For you, I would recommend vacation and luxury rentals because they are much less hands-on. Also, take advantage of the plug-ins I mention over and over. The small up-front cost more than makes up for the freedom that you will have to not only build your business but to enjoy your later years to the fullest.

ACKNOWLEDGMENTS

On behalf of the Landlord Academy team, I want to acknowledge our struggles that helped lead us to writing this book: a brain tumor, debt, a learning disability, unemployment, doubt, fear. Finally, I want to acknowledge the word *impossible,* and expose it for the fraud it is. You see, *impossible* is only a word on the tips of the tongues of men who lack faith. Impossible is nothing.

Very special acknowledgment goes to my loving wife, Lacy, and incredible daughter, Naomi. Someone wiser than me once said to me: You can be the richest man in the world without having a dime in the bank. Now I truly understand.

BONUS PROPERTY MANAGEMENT FORMS

SEVEN-DAY NOTICE TO CURE

TO: _____ and all others in possession

_____

_____

FROM: _____

DATE: _____

You are hereby notified that you are not complying with your lease, specifically that:

1. _____
2. _____
3. _____
4. _____

Demand is hereby given to you in writing that you remedy the noncompliance within seven (7) days of receipt of this notice or your lease shall be deemed terminated, and you shall vacate the premises upon such termination. If this same conduct or conduct of a similar nature is repeated within twelve (12) months, your tenancy is subject to termination without further warning and without your being given an opportunity to cure the noncompliance.

_____

_____

_____

_____

CERTIFICATE OF SERVICE

I certify that a copy of this notice has been furnished to the above-named tenant on _____, 20_____,
at _____ AM/PM by: _____.

1. Delivery.   2. Posting in a conspicuous place on the premises.   3. Certified mail

THREE-DAY NOTICE INSTRUCTIONS

Please follow these tips when completing your three-day notice.

1. **DATE:** The date should be the date you are actually posting or delivering the notice.

2. **TENANT NAME(S):** Write the <u>names of all adult tenants</u> who are actually on the lease or the names of any adult tenants if there is no lease.

3. **ADDRESS:** Write the correct address and county (and apartment number, if any) on the notice.

4. **AMOUNT OF RENT DUE:** This is the <u>actual amount of rent</u> the tenant owes you. <u>DO NOT</u> include any late fees or utilities.

5. **DATE NOTICE EXPIRES:**
   - Do not count the day that the notice is posted or delivered.
   - Do not count any holidays. (Check your county website for court-recognized holidays.)
   - Below is a list of some of the more common dates of holidays recognized in various counties throughout the state of Florida during the 2017 calendar year:
   - 1/2, 1/16, 4/14, 5/29, 7/4, 9/4, 9/21, 11/10, 11/23, 11/24, 12/25, 12/26
   - This list is not exhaustive and you should check with the clerk of court in your county for a list of legal holidays for the year, since each county recognizes different holidays. This link has a list of all the clerks of court in the state to assist you: http://www.flclerks.com/directory.html
   - Do not count Saturdays or Sundays in your calculation.
   - If the notice is posted on Friday, Saturday, or Sunday, day one starts on Monday (unless Monday is a holiday).
   - Do not give less than three days (excluding weekends and holidays).
   - **PO BOXES:** If you are using a PO box as an address for the landlord, you <u>must add five additional business days to the due date in the notice.</u>
   - If your property is located in Brevard, Broward, Citrus, Flagler, Hernando, Lake, Marion, Orange, Osceola, Putnam, Seminole, St. Johns, Sumter, or Volusia County and you live in a different county or state from your tenant, you <u>must add five additional business days to the due date in the notice.</u>

6. **CERTIFICATE OF SERVICE:** Complete the date, time, and person who posted or delivered the notice.

7. **LANDLORD INFORMATION:** Fill in the landlord/owner's name, address, and phone number. If using a property manager or agent, include this information as well.

8. **HOW TO DELIVER THE NOTICE:** The notice should be delivered to the tenant or posted on the door.
   - Do not mail the notice or you <u>must add five additional business days to the due date in the notice.</u>

MAKE COPIES: Make an exact copy of the notice you delivered to the tenant, and keep it for your records. This will be needed to file your lawsuit.

    These instructions and the attached notice are provided for your convenience and should not be construed as legal advice. If you are unsure about what type of notice to post, or how to complete the notice, please contact an attorney.

Date: _____
       (Date notice is delivered)

To: _____ and all others in possession
       (Names of all adult tenants)

_____ Apt _____
       (Property address)

_____, _____, _____
       (City)   *(State)*   *(Zip)*

THREE-DAY NOTICE FOR NONPAYMENT OF RENT

You hereby are notified that you are indebted to me in the sum of $_____ for the rent and

(Excluding utilities and late fees)

use of the premises located at _____ Apt. _____,

(Address of property)   *(Apt. # if any)*

_____, _____, _____, _____,

(City)   *(State)*   *(Zip)*   *(County)*

now occupied by you, and that I demand payment of the rent or possession of the premises within three days (excluding Saturdays, Sundays, and legal holidays) from the date of delivery of this notice, specifically, on or before

_____.

(Date notice expires)

A copy of this notice is being sent to the housing authority to notify them of the termination of your tenancy, via US Mail, to: _____.

(Housing authority address)

CERTIFICATE OF SERVICE

I certify that a copy of this notice has been furnished to the above-named tenant on _____

(Date notice delivered)

20_____, at _____ by _____.

(Time)   *(Name of person who served notice)*

1. Delivery to tenant.
2. Posting in a conspicuous place on the premises.

Landlord Name: _____

Landlord's Agent *(if you are not owner)*: _____

Address: _____

_____

Phone Number: _____

NOTICE OF NONRENEWAL

To: _____
Tenant's Name

_____
Address

_____
City, State, Zip Code

From: _____

Date: _____, 20____

Dear _____,

(Tenant's Name)

You are notified that your tenancy will not be renewed at the end of the present term. You will be expected to vacate the premises on or before _____, 201___. In the event that you do not vacate the premises by said date, legal action may be taken in which you may be held liable for double rent, court costs, and attorney's fees.

CERTIFICATE OF SERVICE

I certify that a copy of this notice has been furnished to the above-named tenant on _____ 20_____, at _____ by _____.

1. Delivery to tenant.
2. Posting in a conspicuous place on the premises.

Landlord's Name _____

Address _____

Phone Number _____

LEASE TERMINATION AGREEMENT

WHEREAS, it is mutually agreed on this _____ day of _____, 20_____, by and between LARRY LANDLORD ("Landlord") and TIMMY TENANT ("Tenant") that the lease described below shall be terminated effective the _____ day of _____, 20_____.

The Landlord hereby agrees that Tenant shall not be held responsible for the covenants and obligations contained in the lease on or after the above effective date. The Landlord and Tenant also agree that Landlord will retain the security deposit of $_____. In consideration thereof, the Tenant hereby agrees to release and surrender all right, title, and interest in and to the lease and Premises described below on the effective date.

If Tenant remains in premises after the agreed-upon vacate date, Tenant will be considered a holdover tenant and will be subject to eviction. Landlord will also be entitled to double rent if Tenant fails to vacate on or before _____, 20_____.

Tenant agrees to leave the Premises in "broom clean" condition and remove any personal property from the Premises and leave all appliances and fixtures in the Premises. Any property or personal possessions remaining in the Premises after _____, 20_____, shall be deemed to be abandoned and Landlord shall be entitled to dispose of them.

By executing this agreement, Tenant agrees that they are forever barred from any and all claims and causes of action, whether known or unknown, that have arisen with regard to the said lease and as of the date of this Agreement. The Parties agree to execute and deliver any additional papers, documents, and other assurances, and take all acts that are reasonably necessary to carry out the intent of this Agreement.

Address of the rental unit ("Premises"): 123 Main Street, Anytown, USA, 12345

Term of the lease being terminated: _____, 20_____, to, _____, 20_____

Date the lease was signed: _____, 20_____

IN WITNESS WHEREOF, Landlord and Tenant have affixed their signatures below on the date first written above.

Landlord or Agent _____

Tenant _____

NOTICE OF TERMINATION OF WEEK-TO-WEEK TENANCY

Date: _____

To: _____ and all others in possession

Address: _____ City, State, Zip _____, FL _____

NOTICE OF TERMINATION OF WEEK-TO-WEEK TENANCY

You are a week-to-week tenant in the premises located at _____, _____, FL _____.

You hereby are notified that pursuant to Chapter 83 Florida Statutes your week-to-week tenancy for the rent and use of the premises located at _____, _____, FL _____, _____ County is being terminated and you are required to vacate the premises and surrender same to your landlord on _____, 20_____.

This notice is being served upon you not less than 7 days prior to the end of the applicable rental period as required by law.

CERTIFICATE OF SERVICE: I certify that a copy of this notice has been furnished to the above-named tenant on _____, 20__, at _____ (a.m.) (p.m.) by: _____.

1. Hand delivery to tenant
2. Posting in a conspicuous place on the premises

Landlord's Name _____

Address _____

City _____, State _____, Zip _____

Phone Number _____

NOTICE OF TERMINATION OF MONTH-TO-MONTH TENANCY

Date: _____

To: _____ and all others in possession

Address: _____ City, State, Zip _____, FL _____

NOTICE OF TERMINATION OF MONTH-TO-MONTH TENANCY

You are a month-to-month tenant in the premises located at _____, _____, FL _____, your rental period beginning on the _____ day of each month.

You hereby are notified that pursuant to Section 83.57 Florida Statutes your month-to-month tenancy for the rent and use of the premises located at _____, _____, FL _____, _____ County is being terminated and you are required to vacate the premises and surrender same to your landlord on _____, 20_____.

This notice is being served upon you not less than fifteen (15) days prior to the end of the applicable rental period as required by law.

A copy of this notice is being sent to the housing authority to notify them of the termination of your tenancy, via U.S. Mail, to: _____.

(Housing authority address)

CERTIFICATE OF SERVICE

I certify that a copy of this notice has been furnished to the above-named tenant on _____, 20_____, at _____ (a.m.) (p.m.) by: _____.

   1. Hand delivery to tenant

   2. Posting in a conspicuous place on the premises

Landlord's Name _____

Address _____

City _____, State _____, Zip _____

Phone Number_____

POOL/SPA ADDENDUM

Tenant(s) _____

_____

Address _____

_____

This lease addendum is incorporated into and made a part of the executed lease for the premises referenced above, and shall be effective upon execution by the parties, hereinafter ("landlord") and ("tenant").

Tenant acknowledges that the subject property has a (swimming pool, spa, and/or hot tub) located thereon. The tenant will use the swimming pool and/or hot tub at the tenant's own risk. Tenant shall release, hold harmless, indemnify, and defend landlord for any and all damages arising out of the use and enjoyment of the pool, including injuries caused to tenant's family, invitees, guests, principals, or licensees to the premises.

At all times, tenant shall be responsible for keeping all gates locked and the swimming pool/hot tub area secured.

The tenant understands and agrees to allow the landlord access at regular times to maintain the pool equipment. The tenant agrees to refrain from attempting to make any repairs or adjustments to the pool equipment or to any of the electrical wiring for the pool equipment.

The tenant must immediately notify the landlord of any repair that the swimming pool/hot tub may require. The tenant is responsible for the full cost that may be due for repair and/or replacement of the swimming pool/hot tub as a result of negligence by the tenant or the tenant's occupants or guests. The tenant must operate the swimming pool/hot tub in accordance with the manufacturer's instructions in a safe, responsible manner.

No pets of any kind are permitted in the swimming pool and/or hot tub at any time.

The tenant understands that the swimming pool and/or hot tub is strictly an amenity and that the use of this amenity is not guaranteed under the terms of the lease. Any interruption or nonavailability of the use of the swimming pool/hot tub will not violate any terms of the lease.

If the tenant violates any part of this addendum, the tenant will then be in default of the lease. In the event of a default, the landlord may initiate legal proceedings in accordance with local and state regulations to evict or have the tenant removed from the leased premises, as well as seek judgment against the tenant for any monies owed to the landlord as a result of the tenant's default.

Tenant(s) _____

Signature _____

Date _____

Landlord/Agent _____

Signature _____

Date _____

INDEX

ABOUT THE AUTHOR

Bryan Chavis is the founder of The Landlord Property Management Academy and also of Chavis Realty and Property Management 365 Franchise, one of the most innovative property management franchises available. Bryan is one of the world's leading property management consultants. His consulting company was awarded the 2016 Best Practice award for Landlord/Property Management Training by FAHRO (Florida Association of Housing and Redevelopment Officials).

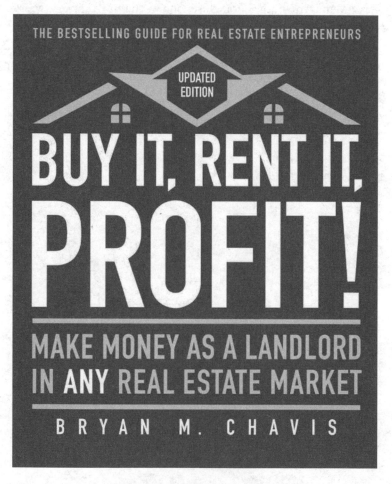